EXCELLER SELECT
TOP PICKS

Empowering BLACK WOMEN *Through* FEMALE SOLIDARITY *in Selected* BLACK FEMALE *Narratives*

Empowering BLACK WOMEN *Through* FEMALE SOLIDARITY *in Selected* BLACK FEMALE *Narratives*

Md Abu Shahid Abdullah

&

Moutushi Islam

EXCELLER BOOKS®
A GLOBAL PRESS

Empowering Black Women through Female Solidarity in
Selected Black Female Narratives

Cover by Exceller Books using resources from Pixabay.com

ISBN: 978-81-19524-07-5

First published in India in 2024 by Exceller Books,
An imprint of GE Group

Address: G1, Dream Apartment, Degree College Road, Belgharia,
Kolkata, 700056, India

EXCELLER BOOKS®
A GLOBAL PRESS

www.excellerbooks.com

Dedicated to

Zohair Rubaiyat Abdullah
&
Mahbubul Islam Khan

Acknowledgement

First and foremost, we are grateful to Allah for granting us the strength and ability to accomplish this task. Secondly, we extend our heartfelt gratitude to our parents and family members for their unwavering faith in us. Lastly, we would like to thank our colleagues for their encouragement and invaluable support.

Table of Contents

| Chapter 1 |

Introduction

God topples from the sky, hell's fire fade:
Exit seraphim and Satan's men:
I shut my eyes and all the world drops dead.
(Plath 10-12)

This stanza from Sylvia Plath's poem *Mad Girl's Love Song* depicts female outrage resulting from the prolonged suppression of women's voices. Although this poem was written from a white woman's perspective, it can still express collective feminine desires and frustration. In comparison to white women, black women are doubly victimized in society because of their identity as women emerging from the black community. As a result, a black woman's expression has often been neglected neglected. However, upon reading several works of black female literature written by black women, we have observed that these black female writers included black women's perspectives to highlight the necessity of black female empowerment. As feminists, they tried to speak for these women by giving them the central position. Regardless of their color or ethnicity, women are given a subservient position by patriarchal society. Nonetheless, these female writers aspired to reconstruct the masculine narrative and express their disagreement concerning the subordinate role of women. As claimed by Cixous, "[w]oman must write her self […]" (875), there is a generous amount of literary work written for women by male writers. However, feminists believe that women should also write for themselves and other women to legitimize their personal experiences as a marginalized group. This concept is directly connected to gynocriticism, a term coined by Elaine Showalter in 1979. Writing is an essential tool to give voice to suppressed women. So, writers supporting gender equality adopt unique strategies to free their work from patriarchal influence. In this book, we will show that black female writers subverted patriarchal narratives to offer agency to their black female protagonists and rose above the impediments caused by patriarchy to reconstruct their lives. These black heroines ensured their emancipation through their rejection of male dominance and the friendship they developed with other black women.

As specimens of black female literature, we have selected five novels titled: *I, Tituba, Black Witch of Salem* by Maryse Condé, *Mama Day* by Gloria Naylor, *The Color Purple* by Alice Walker, *Sassafrass, Cypress & Indigo* by Ntozake Shange and *Beloved* by Toni Morrison. In *I, Tituba, Black Witch of Salem,* the fictional Tituba depicts the victimization of a black female slave. As a young girl, Tituba witnesses the wrongful execution of her mother, Abena, by the patriarchal society. Tituba herself is mutilated by both white and black men. After marriage, Tituba's black husband, John Indian, often calls her 'witch' to denigrate her identity and passively allows his white mistress, Susanna Endicott, to objectify Tituba. Later, the Puritans make Tituba a target of Salem Witch Trial when she moves to Salem with her white master, Samuel Parris, a racial and religious bigot who labels Tituba as 'evil'. Tituba evades her execution by providing a false confession in the Salem court. In the end, Tituba dies as a revolutionary while leading a black revolt against the white planters after returning to her native land, Barbados. The otherworldly knowledge that Tituba receives from a female Shaman, Mama Yaya, helps her (Tituba) survive these ordeals inflicted by the hypocritical society. After her death, Tituba uses her magic to communicate with her chosen progeny, Samantha, to ensure the continuance of resistance among black women against male subjugation. Cocoa, the African American female protagonist in *Mama Day,* succeeds in shaping her future through the challenging phases that nearly threatens her life. Cocoa is raised in Willow Springs by her grandmother, Abigail, and her great-aunt, Miranda, who are an inseparable part of her life. After migrating to New York, Cocoa struggles for seven years to adjust to the modern environment until George's arrival brings a positive change in her monotonous life. George and Cocoa's egalitarian marriage allows her to concentrate on her individual goals. When Cocoa's health deteriorates due to Ruby's sorcery, Miranda uses her superior knowledge to rescue Cocoa. Later, Miranda and Abigail aid Cocoa in recovering emotionally and physically after George's death. As a result, Cocoa efficiently overcomes the obstacles and continues to pursue her ambitions to reconstruct her future. *The Color Purple* narrates the unpleasant experiences of Celie, an African American heroine whose letters to God and her sister, Nettie, reveal the unsettling episodes of her (Celie) life that she eventually surmounts. Celie's adoptive father, Alphonso, and her husband, Albert, exploit her both sexually and emotionally. Initially, Celie endures their abusive behavior and writes to God for comfort. Nonetheless, she observes how Harpo's wife, Sofia, and Albert's lover, Shug, deny patriarchal domination. Eventually, Celie develops self-awareness that enables her to resist male control like Sofia and Shug. In due course, Celie reclaims her self-esteem through her friendship with Shug, Nettie, and Sofia. Celie learns to defend her dignity against Albert's hypocritical attitude and rejects her unhappy marriage with him. Once a silent sufferer, Celie becomes self-aware and travels to Memphis with Shug to establish her (Celie's) distinct identity. The introductory letters of *The Color Purple* document Celie's afflicted voice. However, Celie's voice resonates with self-contentment when she concludes her letter writing as a successful businesswoman, thriving amidst her family. *Sassafrass, Cypress & Indigo* tells the (hi)story of the Effania family, showing the individual struggle and development of the Effania sisters – Sassafrass, Cypress and Indigo. By mixing recipes, poems and cartographies, Shange associates each sister's life story with their family history and the history of African Americans. The stories of the three sisters, encountering contradictory expectations, traditions and neo/postcolonial experiences, reveal their search for voice and identity as women, artists, daughters and social and political activists. The Effania sisters are storytellers and conjurers, possessing great skills of being connected with larger black worlds as in the slave communities imagined by Indigo. *Beloved* portrays a dark and powerful picture of the dehumanizing effects of slavery and focuses on the power of memory and history; part of Morrison's plan in the novel is to recover a history that has been destroyed by forced silence and deliberate forgetfulness. The story of the protagonist Sethe and her two daughters, Beloved and Denver, stands against the official history of white slave owners and slave traders, which ignored and, more specifically, silenced many horrifying personal histories of the slaves in the United States. This suppression and dissociation from the past by the slaves, in an attempt to erase the brutal memories of slavery, causes a disintegration of self and a loss of true identity. By using the magical realist technique, Morrison attempts to provide an alternative version of history, a version that was told by the slaves, the oppressed, and the un-represented, to that supported by the dominant power.

Apart from the introductory and concluding chapters, we have dedicated five chapters to five novels that incorporate distinct theoretical frameworks to support our arguments. In the second chapter, titled "Magical Realism and Female Solidarity in Maryse Condé's *I, Tituba, Black Witch of Salem,*" we will demonstrate Tituba's struggles to ensure the continuance of black resistance amongst her own people before her execution by the white planters. From her own point of view, the fictional Tituba records sufferings at the hands of stereotypical men and white supremacists. We will attempt to argue that the magical realist elements present in *I, Tituba, Black Witch of Salem* grant the fictional Tituba a voice to dismantle the pre-existing patriarchal narrative that treats the expressions of the oppressed women with indifference. Elaine Showalter's theoretical framework of gynocriticism delineates the significance of writing produced by women to provide their perspectives with a just treatment. On the other hand, magical realism is a narrative mode that is used by marginalized and cross-cultural female writers to speak for themselves and their female readers. Patricia Hart, who coins the term 'magical feminism', talks about female voices in magical realist narratives that can depict their position in literary work. For this reason, we will use the understandings of Showalter and Hart to support our first argument. Tituba's knowledge regarding the supernatural enables her to maintain a bond with her female ancestors, Mama Yaya and Abena. Learning medicinal knowledge from Mama Yaya enables Tituba to transcend both sexual and racial violence. Tituba uses magic to summon the spirits of Mama Yaya and Abena whenever she requires their guidance. After her death, Tituba sustains a similar connection with Samantha to carry on her (Tituba's) unfinished agenda to transcend patriarchal barriers. We will show that Maryse Condé takes the support of magical realist narrative mode to demonstrate the importance of female unity for their emancipation as a collective. The communication Mama Yaya, Abena and Tituba maintain between them through magic develops into a friendship. This shared affinity empowers Tituba to initiate the subversion of male subjugation, which impedes the growth of black women. In the book *Magic(al) Realism,* Maggie Ann Bowers provides her understanding of magical realism used by the authors in her writings. According to Bowers, many feminist writers incorporate magical realist writing techniques to express themselves for their ability to transgress and challenge the typical norms. We will draw a magical realist analysis to argue that female friendship works as an instrument to alter Tituba's identity as a victim.

In the third chapter, "Achieving Individual Transformation and Securing a Peaceful Future in Gloria Naylor's *Mama Day,*" we will assess the factors that facilitate the continuation of Cocoa's individual growth. Cocoa's husband, George, portrays a character uninfluenced by patriarchal prejudices. Cocoa can exert equal authority in her marriage to retain her individuality. After marriage, George does not interrupt Cocoa when she decides to complete her higher studies before having children and continuing to work. As a result, Cocoa and George's bond questions a traditional marriage in which the dominating husband controls the choices of his wife. According to Susan Arndt, black feminism challenges patriarchal assumptions and offers choices to the oppressed black women to alter their subjugation. We shall apply Arndt's findings to argue that Cocoa succeeds in accomplishing her personal goals after marriage without facing any patriarchal barrier because of the reformist male-female relationship she shares with George. Cocoa's grandmothers, Miranda and Abigail, are responsible for shaping her personality. They provide Cocoa with guidance and comfort during the tough phases of her life. Miranda's magical ability saves Cocoa from Ruby's possession. Miranda performs a mystic ritual to break Ruby's curse. Later, Abigail and Miranda use herbal remedies to restore Cocoa's health. After George's death, they (Miranda and Abigail) console Cocoa and motivate her to reformulate her future. Without the presence of any male superior in Day's family, the matriarchs, Miranda and

Abigail, efficiently secure Cocoa's future, a feat which establishes that having male support is not an absolute necessity for Miranda, Abigail and Cocoa to ensure an optimistic future for their family. Bowers demonstrate the ability of magical realist writing to subvert the unverifiable aspects and attack the prevalent norms. We will incorporate Bowers' concept to prove that Cocoa's matriarchal family challenges male authority and suggests the efficiency of female friendship in empowering an afflicted woman. During Cocoa and George's visit to Willow Springs, Ruby casts a dark spell that threatens Cocoa's life. Kimberly Springer argues that black women can hinder their progress as a collective if they compete for status instead of supporting one another. We will use Springer's findings to analyze Ruby's jealousy towards Cocoa. Ruby's evildoing takes George's life and endangers Cocoa's future, whereas Miranda and Abigail's affection and support recover Cocoa from the damage Ruby causes in her life. So, we can say that the contrast between Cocoa's progressive bond with her grandmothers and Ruby's detrimental rivalry with Cocoa in the novel signifies the importance of unity among black women to ensure their emancipation.

In the fourth chapter of this project, "Female Friendship and Rejection of Male Supremacy in Alice Walker's *The Color Purple,*" we will analyze how the protagonist of *The Color Purple,* Celie, completely transforms from a passive being to a self-righteous woman through the support received from other black women. Celie observes Shug's tendency to use satirical expressions every now and then to derogate Albert's presumed manliness. Indicating Albert's lack of control over her, Shug uses the word 'weak' to insult his manhood. Similarly, when Celie finds her own voice to resist Albert's dominance, she calls him a "lowdown dog" (Walker 180). Later, Celie compares Albert to a frog to insult his hypocritical attitude. In the book *All Joking Aside: American Humor and Its Discontents*, Rebecca Krefting explains how the 'Jokesters' challenge the existing social inequality by transgressing the dominant ideology through comic expressions and jokes. Evaluating Celie and Shug's choice of words on the basis of Krefting's perspective, we will argue that these black women take the support of parody to challenge presumed male values. Celie develops a strong affinity towards Shug, which is completely opposite to how he (Celie) feels for men. Celie and Shug's shared affection eventually takes a sexual and romantic turn. Ti-Grace Atkinson considers lesbianism as one of the ways for oppressed women to resist male dominance. Hence, Celie's homosexual interest can be observed as an attempt to deny male influence in her life. Based on Krefting and Atkinson's understandings, we will argue that the satirical remarks of black women towards men and Celie's homosexual tendency in *The Color Purple* serve to oppose male prejudices. Moreover, according to Jennifer Hamer and Helen Neville, oppressed black women can develop mutual empathy based on their common experiences as the victims of a patriarchal society. Their shared understanding of each other's sufferings can form an alliance to resist male oppression as a collective. Acknowledging Hamer and Neville's black feminist observation, we will emphasize that the sense of sisterhood between Shug, Celie, Nettie and

Sofia is influenced by their shared empathy, which ensures their empowerment as a group. Celie's friendship inspires her to evaluate her passive approach towards life and resist male oppression to reclaim her individuality. However, the motivation Celie receives from other black women cannot ensure her progress unless she realizes her self-worth and puts an effort to bring positive changes in her life. Celie's friendship with other black women would have been insufficient to ensure her personal growth without her self-initiated attempts.

In the fifth chapter, "Searching for Female Identity and Freedom in Ntozake Shange's *Sassafrass, Cypress & Indigo,*" we will show how the act of reclaiming black women's artistic and political subjectivity is interwoven with unresolved domestic tensions. We will demonstrate how Shange attempts to give black women a voice through spirituality, establish alternative mode(s) of storytelling, and reconstruct history from a marginalized (here, female) standpoint where creating and living in an alternative reality enables Indigo to overthrow the dominant social order. By emphasizing the lives of black women, Shange demonstrates how art – music, dance and weaving – plays a significant role in female emancipation and self-expression, particularly how music works as a unifying factor among black people. Cypress's incarnation of the black women's heritage through her body movement, something that Sassafrass does with her reconceived weaving and/or writing, and her invocation of the history as "Yanvallou" and "Damballa's child" reflects the Southern magic traditions of Indigo, suggesting the fact that Cypress is able to come to terms with her previously ignored legacy and direct it to recover her artistic self and identity. It is through her dance that she speaks up, breaking her earlier silence. We will also argue that Shange shows the black slaves' connection with spirituality as a way of seeking solace for their suffering and escaping their bitter lives. The renewed magic and the history of black people are the driving forces for recovering and sharing their collective experiences that would ultimately earn them political agency. By filling in the gap between a lost history and her very own black community, Indigo plays a significant role in reforming such common experiences.

In the sixth chapter, "Rewriting Identity Loss and Asserting Female Solidarity in Toni Morrison's *Beloved,*" we will argue how Morrison seems to base her magical realism on the belief system of the African American cultural group. Her stories are strongly influenced by African American oral culture and mythology. In *Beloved,* she uses the magical realist technique to talk about the cruelty of slavery, reinterpret the official history of white slave owners and put an alternative history from the perspective of the slaves. It is not only the story of the protagonist Sethe, who kills her daughter to save her from the cruelty of slavery, but also the composite story of all slaves and their quest for freedom, and even of those who died in the 'Middle Passage' during their journey by slave ships. Morrison uses the magical realist device of a ghost named Beloved, who is the embodiment of collective memories of the black community and who, by reminding Sethe and other ex-black slaves of their past, allows them to tell their own story and create their own version of history, and thus enables them to assert their identity which is lost through slavery. By dealing with historical issues critically and trying to cure historical wounds, magical realism in the novels mirrors history as well as strives to change it.

We will show that the female protagonists of the five analyzed novels reach the common goal of subverting patriarchal oppression and reconstructing their individual identities by utilizing diverse tactics. In *I, Tituba, Black Witch of Salem,* Tituba uses magic to create a link with both her female ancestors and successors to ensure the continuity of black female resistance. Cocoa secures her individuality by forming a positive and progressive bond with a male partner who does not conform to the twisted patriarchal ideologies in *Mama Day*. On the other hand, Celie, Sofia, Shug and Mary Agnes, the black female characters of *The Color Purple,* attack toxic masculinity by using female humour and forming an alliance among themselves. Again, the three sisters in *Sassafrass, Cypress & Indigo* attempt to change the oppressed condition of black women and rewrite history through art and spirituality. Last but not least, Sethe in *Beloved* attempts to create an alternative version of history by including many excluded stories of black slaves, creating a bond among black people, particularly the female ones, and giving them a voice and, therefore, an identity. Being themselves black women and writing about black women, the writers of these five novels focused on manifold ways which may all lead to black women's freedom. Our book will focus on how these black female writers amalgamated diverse methods to show the emancipation of the black female protagonists and advocate for the idea of sisterhood or female solidarity in their narratives.

| Chapter 2 |

Magical Realism and Female Solidarity in Maryse Condé's *I, Tituba, Black Witch of Salem*

"I can look for my story among those of the witches of Salem, but it isn't there."

(Condé 149)

In her novel *I, Tituba, Black Witch of Salem,* Maryse Condé reconstructs the story of a black Caribbean slave woman with her imagination. Condé's protagonist is denied a place in documented history and is negatively portrayed due to her skin tone and gender. In this novel, the fictional Tituba is given a voice so that she can retell the historical Tituba's story from a survivor's perspective. Tituba's story is ignored and unwritten in history because she is a woman of color. However, the fictional Tituba challenges the validity of the documented history by narrating her story from a first-person viewpoint. Tituba takes control of the narrative to provide the readers with an alternate perspective that is not manipulated either by patriarchy or white supremacy. The novel starts with Tituba mentioning how she is conceived as a product of rape and a representative of colonial, racial and gender-based violence. Since childhood, Tituba has witnessed and endured the mutilation of her family, her fellow Africans, and herself. As a black slave woman, she is often reduced to being an object and termed evil. Nevertheless, Tituba learns to use magic for healing and communicate with the spirits under Mama Yaya's guidance. Acquiring this mystical knowledge enables the victimized Tituba to resist oppression and die as a revolutionary. Condé uses the magical realist narrative technique to propose that black women can alter their subservient position if they are encouraged and provided the relevant tools.

In an interview, Condé was asked about her interpersonal relationship with Tituba, the protagonist of her novel. In reply, Condé said that she was so intensely engaged in an interaction with Tituba that she felt Tituba's presence when writing the novel (qtd. in Condé 200). Furthermore, when Condé was asked whether she was inspired by Arthur Miller's play, *The Crucible*, she remarked on the typical ignorance of a white male writer regarding a black woman's perspective. Elaine Showalter reflects on the limitation of male writing in depicting female experience in a branch of feminist study termed gynocriticism. Showalter states, "Beyond androgyny, women have a lot to say" (353). In other words, the patriarchal narrative cannot entirely represent the female psyche. Additionally, Bell Hooks, in her book *AIN'T I A WOMAN: Black Women and Feminism* writes that literature about black women is often laden with both sexist and racist remarks. Even black men's writings on black women are manipulated by their sexist supposition, and the 19th-century black women's writings are revised by the whites (10). So, a black woman is required to insert her own understanding in writing to assert her individual identity, which is why, in *I, Tituba*[1], Condé adopts Tituba's voice to convey her emotions to the readers. In the novel, Tituba takes control of the narrative to tell her undocumented story, which receives indifferent treatment from the male-dominated society. However, Condé finds no historical existence of the real Tituba from Salem Witch Trial apart from the mention of "a slave originating from the West Indies and probably practising 'hoodoo'" (qtd. in Condé 215). Therefore, she uses the magical realist narrative technique to go beyond factual reality and create a fictional history of Tituba. Patricia Hart coins the term "magical feminism" to set out "magical realism employed in a femino-centric work, or one that is especially insightful into the status or condition of women in the context described in the work" (qtd. in Blackwell 141). In *I, Tituba,* Tituba is a black female 'witch' who is condemned by several demographic groups of society – white males, white females, puritans, black males and even white children whom she nurses back to good health with her heartfelt affection and medicinal knowledge. To cope with this alienation, Tituba creates an alternative reality through magic to establish a connection with other subjugated women in the narrative. In this chapter, we will argue that in *I, Tituba,* black female writing subverts the patriarchal narrative to prioritize the suppressed voices. We will also attempt to prove that magical realism validates Tituba's existence as opposed to the historical 'non-existence' of a black female victim of the infamous Salem

[1] From now on, we will write *I, Tituba* as a short form of *I, Tituba, Black Witch of Salem.*

Witch Trial and consequently turns her into a collective consciousness against the male-dominated society. Furthermore, we will focus on Tituba's interaction with other female characters to prove that sharing their frustrations and experiences with one another establishes a female support system and solidarity between them.

From the very beginning, Condé gives Tituba absolute control of her story as a first-person narrator, which is evident in the novel's title, *I, Tituba, Black Witch of Salem*. In the title, which reads like a statement, Tituba asserts her individual identity by initially mentioning her own name and then letting the readers know the identity that is imposed upon her by society. Tituba is born as a slave and a result of rape when being doubly marginalized both as a black and a woman. She defines the source of her birth as an "act of hatred and contempt" (3), and through this comment, Tituba reflects on her frustration toward the violence done to her mother, Abena, by a white male. According to Araújo, Tituba's antagonism toward white male authoritarianism originates as "a legitimate defensive reaction to harassment and abuse" (223). Tituba is only seven when she sees her mother being unjustly hanged because of a crime she does not commit. However, in Tituba's words, Abena is only trying to protect herself from the attempt of sexual assault by the white man. Tituba watches her mother's dead body hanging from the tree. She describes her trauma by repeatedly uttering, "They hanged my mother" (8). This reference makes it evident that Condé utilizes a first-person narrative voice to express Tituba's personal and intimate emotions. As a first-person storyteller, Tituba authenticates the intensity of her grief.

She acknowledges that the "terror and mourning" (8) that she feels within herself after witnessing Abena's execution has a lasting impact on her. Tituba's mother suffers because she is a black slave woman. So, Abena's story represents colonial brutality. Tituba also narrates the misfortune of the slaves in Barbados in detail, "I saw men go home covered in blood, their chests and backs striped in scarlet" (7). Her description challenges the narrative of the white colonizers, giving an insight into the insufferable oppression endured by the black slaves. Therefore, by taking control of the narrative, Tituba scrutinizes colonial violence while demonstrating the mutilation of the African people by the white planters.

Tituba communicates her consciousness to the readers through her first-person narration, which has no place in the history written by the colonizers. *I, Tituba* rejects white male superiority through a feminist remark by Mama Yaya, an influential black female character, "…man is not the master riding through his kingdom on horseback" (9). This Nago woman provides Tituba with a shelter and helps her to survive. After Mama Yaya's death, Tituba isolates herself from a community dominated by men, specifically 'white' men. Tituba states that, during that time, she was happy (11), which expresses her capability to grow while staying away from the plantations, free from the oppression of the planters. Nevertheless, the novel does not suggest that Tituba needs any man for her survival. Rather, a black man, John Indian's arrival indicates a catastrophic turn in her life through Abena's repetitive weeping, "Why can't women do without men?" (15). Mentioning the fate of the so-called 'witch trial' of

Salem, Dukats argues, "The witch craze was, in fact, a campaign of terrorization against women who exhibited power or defined themselves outside the parameters that patriarchy had set" (747). This resonates with both Mama Yaya and Abena's warning toward Tituba to create her own identity, free from the influence of men. In the novel, John Indian addresses Tituba as "a little witch" (Condé 17), a remark she finds derogatory. In response to John Indian's comment, Tituba defines a 'witch' as a person with an ability to "[…] heal, a superior gift of nature that inspires respect, admiration, and gratitude […]" (17). John Indian uses the term 'witch' to offend Tituba's dignity. Later, John Indian expresses his desire to refute society's claim that Tituba is a witch by accepting her as "my [his] woman" and teaching her prayers (18). Through his statement, John Indian indirectly objectifies Tituba as socially unacceptable because she is a 'witch' and not a Christian. Tituba's acknowledgement, "I knew I should have fled" (18), indicates that John Indian makes Tituba feel controlled almost the same way as the white men, validating Mama Yaya's earlier claim, "Men do not love. They possess. They subjugate" (14). Nevertheless, Tituba fails to subdue her desire for John Indian and accompanies him to Carlisle Bay, a residence of the whites. However, she admits that it is an act of "Madness and betrayal" (19) because both her mother and adoptive father are mutilated by white men. Tituba is powerless against her longing for John Indian, but she denounces the white male authority by confessing her "Remorse. Shame. Panic. Fear" (20) before moving to the white community.

Tituba's encounter with Susanna Endicott depicts the victimization of Tituba by a white woman. Tituba uses her voice to portray Susanna's attempt to use her presumed superior status in society as a weapon to oppress Tituba. When it comes to the marginalization of women by the patriarchal society, we categorize all women in one group as victims. However, black females are often objectified by white females on the basis of the assumed racial hierarchy. Although white men turn slavery into an institution, the white women benefit from a new "hierarchical social status," which is a direct result of slavery. The white mistresses treat the black men and women inhumanly to sustain their status and assert their superiority over the black slaves (hooks 153). In the novel, Tituba deciphers Susanna's mistreatment toward her by articulating, "She stared at me as if I were an object of disgust" (Condé 21). It is apparent in Tituba's words that Susanna Endicott discriminates against Tituba based on her skin color, as Susanna orders Tituba not to touch her food "with the discolored, waxy palms" (21). Furthermore, Susanna and her friends objectify Tituba during their conversation, ignoring Tituba's presence at the door. Their treatment makes Tituba feel like an outcast, unworthy to have an existence as Tituba describes, "They were striking me off the map of human beings [...]. Tituba only existed insofar as these women let her exist" (24). Tituba narrates that these white women make her feel non-existent, powerless and menial. By expressing her feelings, Tituba depicts the inability of white women to treat black women with respect. In *I, Tituba,* her voice advocates for the injustice and othering done to black women by the white women in the novel. So, Tituba, as the narrator of her story, categorizes herself as more vulnerable than the white women in society.

Tituba's writing stresses the white community's tendency to distort the truth. In *I, Tituba,* Susanna asks Tituba whether she is the daughter of Abena, the lady who murders a planter (26). Tituba opposes Susanna's question by replying, "She didn't kill him. ... Just wounded him" (26). Tituba's narration highlights the fact that she has to 'correct' Susanna's idea as her question indicates that Abena's tragedy is altered to represent the white man as a victim when, in truth, Abena is the victim of the planter's sexual assault. Moreover, Abena does not kill the planter but rather injures him in her defence. So, Tituba's own expression helps the readers to understand that her actual story cannot be accurately portrayed through the lens of white patriarchy. According to Cixous, "I write woman: woman must write woman" (877). Therefore, a black woman, especially Tituba herself, is required to tell the readers about her sufferings for an unadulterated representation of her condition.

Tituba unravels her sufferings as a black woman while living in a Puritan community under the subjugation of her new master, Samuel Parris. She is disapproved of and disregarded by society because she is a non-Christian, black slave woman. Consequently, Tituba becomes the victim of othering done by both white men and children. Tituba's description of Parris's treatment depicts her suffering as a victim of religious bigotry. Depending on Tituba's statement, Samuel Parris is a racist and religious extremist. In describing Parris' aversion to black skin color,

Tituba quotes him, "I know that the color of your skin is the sign of your damnation [...]" (Condé 41). As stated by Parris, black skin apparently symbolizes the evil. Therefore, Tituba is not accepted in the Puritan society. In Parris' home, Tituba is also tormented because of her non-Christian identity. In the novel, Tituba describes that Parris forces her to recite Christian prayers, and when Tituba refuses, he hits her (41). Tituba suffers physical violence because of her supposed inferior status as a black female slave and a religious minority, whereas Parris misuses his assumed supremacy as a Christian white male to victimize Tituba. In response to the forceful recitation of prayers, Tituba says, "Why should I confess? What goes on in my head and my heart is my business" (41). Her articulation questions the self-righteousness of the Puritans and portrays her agony in unwillingly saying the prayers that she neither understands nor believes in. Rahming interprets this behaviour as a Puritan stereotype by remarking on their limited knowledge:

> *[B]y reducing the universe to the limited contents of their puritan consciousness – in effect adhering to essentialist notions of moral and social reality – these villagers accept as certain and irrefutable the epistemological structures that both derive from and undergird this worldview [...] their way of knowing is predicated not on the pliability of experience but on the rigidity of puritan dogma. (28)*

Therefore, Tituba is not inherently an evil witch; rather, the Puritans abuse their religious doctrine to portray her negatively. Additionally, Tituba is addressed disrespectfully by a white child, Abigail, the minister's niece. The way Abigail addresses Tituba as a "Poor, ignorant Negress" is dehumanizing (Condé 44). Tituba is so much neglected in society that she is not even spared the victimization caused by a white child. Thus, Tituba's account of her experiences in Boston reveals the objectification, physical and verbal abuse she receives from both white men and children – truths that a white narrative would have ignored.

Tituba's unbearable suffering becomes vivid as she mentions the self-performed abortion of her child and elaborates on the reason behind killing her child in the womb. She tells her readers about the execution of an old woman accused of being a witch. After witnessing this injustice committed against another woman, Tituba is compelled to recall her mother's execution. She conveys her trauma through her speech, "[…] I felt the desire to scream […] out my suffering, my revolt, and my powerless rage. What kind of a world was this that had turned me into a slave, an orphan, and an outcast?" (Condé 49). Her expression gives away her frustration over the indifferent world that determines such misfortune for someone like her. She questions the legitimacy of the basis on which people like her are enslaved and categorized as rejects to suffer throughout their lives. Even little Abigail claims that the death penalty is deserved by the old woman (49). Shortly after this incident, Tituba decides to terminate her pregnancy as she declares, "There is no happiness in motherhood for a slave" (50). Since childhood, Tituba has seen other slaves kill their infants to spare them from the misery that they endure as slaves. According to Abdullah,

"[…] a slave, who has no identity, the acts of suicide, abortion and infanticide are all various forms of resistance and assertions of suppressed identity" (89). So, abortion can be evaluated as Tituba's reaction to the brutality of slavery. It can be observed as her resistance against slavery, preventing it from infecting her future generation. As the readers go through the phases of Tituba's life, the torment of black women becomes more pronounced to them. Similarly, it can be observed that if a third-person narrator replaces Tituba, an authentic representation of her grief and suffering would have been lost.

Tituba provides her perspective as a victim while scrutinizing the judges of Salem as the actual evils, corrupting the ideology of the community. After Tituba arrives in Salem, people start identifying her as "Satan's deputy" (Condé 71). Ironically, the Puritans are the ones spreading actual evil in the society by subjugating and brainwashing the women and children. In that regard, Tituba stresses the Puritans' attempt to involve children in their conspiracy against the blacks. Tituba quotes Betsey, "You're a Negress, Tituba. … You are evil itself" (77). Ironically, Tituba's narration reveals no legitimate cause for the whites to objectify her as a 'Negress' while associating this supposed derogatory identity with evil. It is hypocritical of the Puritans to twist meaning to persecute black women. Additionally, the Puritans sexually assault Tituba to get a false confession from her. Tituba depicts this atrocity in her narrative voice, "One of the men sat squarely astride me and began to hammer my face with his fists. … Another lifted up my skirt and thrust a sharpened stick into the most sensitive part of my body" (91). Tituba is afflicted by this physical abuse and sexual assault since she is tagged as an "Antichrist" (91). Tituba's description of the assault criticizes the feigned 'morality' of the Puritans. Later, Tituba provides a confession as anticipated by Samuel Parris (106). After her trial in Salem court, Goodwife Parris visits Tituba, where she is kept chained in a barn. Goodwife admits to Tituba that she is misguided and acknowledges the witch trial as "A plot by Parris and his followers" (107). Furthermore, Tituba addresses Judge Danforth as a "filthy racist" (109). Tituba's narration suggests that the Salem Witch Trial is a result of both racial and religious bigotry. Hooks explains, "The Salem Witchcraft Trials were an extreme expression of patriarchal society's persecution of women. They were a message to all women that unless they remained within passive, subordinate roles, they would be punished, even put to death" (30). Likewise, Tituba's storytelling implies that she is not doing any evil through witchcraft. Rather, this false claim is used as an excuse to mutilate the blacks, particularly the black women, as they are the weaker target. Therefore, she is a victim whose only fault is to be born as a black woman.

Tituba differentiates her life as more ill-fated than a black man by demonstrating the misfortune that she endures as a black woman. She is objectified and abandoned by her black lover, John Indian. Tituba says that he would not have hesitated to tag her as a 'witch' for his own survival if the situation demanded (Condé 110). Ironically, while Tituba struggles with her life, John Indian somehow escapes the oppression. Tituba laments, "Good for the gallows, I was wearing myself out in bondage while my man was striding around his new estate in leather boots with a conquering air and assessing his wealth" (130). Tituba is persecuted, imprisoned and enslaved, whereas John Indian marries his mistress, one of the richest white women in town. Tituba draws the comparison between her life and John Indian's life to show that Tituba suffers more than him as she is a black woman. Moreover, after returning to Barbados, Tituba is mistreated by another black man, Christopher. Tituba narrates how he insults her by addressing Tituba as nobody special but an ordinary "Negress" to expect a special treatment (155). The word 'negress' is used by the whites to dehumanize Tituba. Now, the same word is used by Christopher to entitle her as inferior to him. Later, the black resistance against the planters fail and Tituba is executed on account of Christopher's betrayal. Tituba's relationship with John Indian and Christopher demonstrate the maltreatment she receives from black men. It indicates that black women cannot expect security, respect or support even from black men. In describing the marginalization of black women in the white community, Frances M. Beal uses the term "double jeopardy" and claims, "[…] the black woman in America can justly be described as a 'slave of a slave'" (168). In Beal's words, the women are doubly exploited by the white colonizers and their white mistresses since the objectified black men can still sustain their patriarchal domination on black women. Similarly, *I, Tituba* depicts the mutilation of Tituba by the black male slaves alongside the white masters. So, having the authority over her story, Tituba portrays the discrimination that a black woman faces within her own community.

Tituba's first-person narration depicts the hostile situation endured by black women in every layer of society, which we have analyzed so far in this chapter. Tituba is a victim of male prejudice, white supremacy and slavery. Nonetheless, Tituba resists her victimization through her friendship with other women. Tituba is raised by a shaman, Mama Yaya, who shares her supernatural knowledge with Tituba. Mama Yaya's teachings enable Tituba to use magic for healing and self-assertion. Both Mama Yaya and Abena's spirits guide Tituba as she tries to challenge her misfortune. Later, when Tituba decides to terminate her unwanted pregnancy using 'herbal properties', Mama Yaya's friend, Old Judah, mysteriously appears to rekindle Tituba's magical abilities. Evidently, Condé incorporates magical realism with female solidarity to subvert the 'traditional' patriarchal reality and create an alternative narrative which favours women's intimate emotions and desires. The magical realist writing technique used by Condé in this novel acts as a shield against racial and patriarchal oppressions, allowing Tituba to assert her own individuality from the perspective of an oppressed minority – a black woman living under the dual domination of colonialism and patriarchy. According to Bowers, "The characteristic of magical realism which makes it such a frequently adopted narrative mode is its inherent transgressive and subversive qualities. It is this feature that has led many post-colonial, feminist and cross-cultural writers to embrace it as a means of expressing their ideas" (63). In *I, Tituba,* magical realism acts as a tool to dismantle the patriarchal depiction of a black woman. The patriarchal society entitles Tituba as a 'witch' in an attempt to disregard her individuality. Interestingly, the term 'witch' itself is a feminine one, indicating that, consciously or subconsciously, the patriarchal society associates supernatural ability with women. This tendency of the white male colonizers essentially otherizes women, especially black women, from the privileged social class. As a reaction, the magical realist technique unifies the subjugated female voices by creating an alternate narrative space for them to sororize, heal and grow. In the next section of this chapter, we shall interpret Tituba's reliance on female spirits and supernatural healing to argue that, in *I, Tituba,* magical realism acts as a link between generations of subjugated black women to break the cycle of their endurance.

Mama Yaya's guidance and inspiration provide Tituba with a scope of self-exploration. Mama Yaya shelters Tituba, a seven-year-old orphan, when she is expelled from the plantation. Having no guardian, Tituba would have failed to survive without the "solidarity among slaves" (Condé 8). Tituba is not a direct descent of Mama Yaya. However, the ancestral connection between them is sealed by the sufferings they endure as black women. Like Tituba's parents, Mama Yaya's husband and sons are "tortured to death" (8) by the whites. So, Mama Yaya and Tituba share a mutual understanding of grief. Mama Yaya herself is an outcast because of her association with the supernatural. Nevertheless, her powers enable her to help the people in need. Mama Yaya uses her metaphysical ability to determine her own identity and aids Tituba in asserting herself by sharing her knowledge. Mama Yaya's words, "You will suffer during your life. ... But you'll survive" (9), motivate Tituba throughout her life. Her experience empowers her to guide young Tituba. During her lifetime, Mama Yaya witnesses the ability of white men to terrorize the slaves. In that regard, she suggests Tituba resist male authority as Tituba deserves respect like everyone else (9). By teaching Tituba about the healing properties found in herbs, Mama Yaya passes down her ancestral wisdom to help Tituba survive the odds. Mama Yaya's remark, "The dead only die if they die in our hearts [...]. A few words are enough to conjure them back and [...] to make themselves useful" (10), indicates the capability of the forebears to lead and support their children. Instructed by Mama Yaya, Tituba uses her powers to heal and console her own people. Accordingly, she acquires the opportunity to be 'seen' and understood by them. Mama Yaya fails to accomplish certain things in life. Nonetheless, the journey ahead of Tituba is secured by the insights into life that Mama Yaya provides her. After Mama Yaya's demise, her spirit continues to communicate with Tituba to offer her guidance, inspiration and comfort. In Tituba's venture for emancipation, Mama Yaya prevents her from being consumed by revenge and advises her to heal people through her powers (29). Tituba's statement, "Mama Yaya [convinced] me that in the end nothing would be able to destroy me. In short, Mama Yaya brought me hope [...]" (84), indicates her contribution to transforming Tituba into a resolute woman. Therefore, Mama Yaya's affinity for Tituba helps her defy the victimization of herself and other black women as a collective.

The exchange of acknowledgement between Tituba and Elizabeth Parris unites them for mutual support.

Elizabeth is Tituba's mistress and the wife of Samuel Parris. Despite belonging to the privileged social class, Goodwife Parris is subjugated by her husband as she is a woman. On the other hand, Samuel Parris dominates Tituba as his slave. So, Tituba and Elizabeth find a mutual ground to share compassion with each other. Upon first meeting, Elizabeth expresses her understanding of Tituba's misery by saying, "How cruel it must be to be separated from your own family. From your father, mother, and your people" (Condé 38). Elizabeth's pleasant remark surprises Tituba as she did not receive such a gesture of compassion from her former mistress, Susanna Endicott. Eventually, Tituba identifies Elizabeth as a victim like herself, and concedes, "I couldn't tell who was the more distressed, the more terrified, Mistress Parris or myself" (39). The comprehensibility of each other's sufferings takes the form of sisterhood between Tituba and Elizabeth. Elizabeth's daughter, Betsey, soon becomes a part of their alliance. Tituba's comment, "We [Elizabeth, Betsey and Tituba] devised a thousand tricks to be together in the absence of this devil, the Reverend Mr. Parris" (41), indicates that they find comfort in their friendship. The affection shown by both Elizabeth and Betsey makes Tituba feel recognized. In return, Tituba nurtures them with her care. When Elizabeth's health deteriorates, Tituba "calls on the supernatural" (45) to cure her. Likewise, during Tituba's emotional breakdown after terminating her pregnancy, Elizabeth and Betsey "increases their attentions" (52) to comfort her. Additionally, Tituba finds a way to redeem the murder of her unborn child when she heals Betsey from illness in Salem. While rinsing Betsey with the healing water, Tituba says, "[...] I was purifying myself of the murder of my child" (63). So, Elizabeth, Betsey and Tituba's bonding is reciprocal. Whitehead writes, "Male violence and coercive forms of heterosexuality leading to violence, rape and wife-battering and issues surrounding reproduction and mothering [...] provide women with an explicit basis for gender solidarity" (6). Although Elizabeth is not a black slave woman like Tituba, nevertheless she is also a victim of Samuel's patriarchal domination in the form of domestic violence, which enables Tituba to empathize with her and, in turn, build a mutual friendship. Despite this bonding, their attachment declines once the Parris family settles in Salem due to Samuel Parris' conspiracy against Tituba. Nevertheless, the temporary place of relief and support that Tituba, Elizabeth and Betsey partake transform Tituba. It enables her to survive the trauma inflicted by Samuel Parris.

Tituba's brief and mysterious encounter with Judah White assures her that she contributes to a society ruled by men. Old Judah is Mama Yaya's friend and a female healer like her. In Boston, Tituba witnesses the unjust persecution of women who are suspected as 'witches'. Traumatized by this misfortune of slaves, Tituba acknowledges her "sad existence" (Condé 50) and considers aborting her child. Tituba's lack of knowledge about the plants found in Boston puts her in a difficult situation in picking the exact herbs required for her scheme. Judah White makes her enigmatic appearance in Tituba's assistance. Old Judah teaches Tituba "the names and properties" (51) of the plants that grow in the forests of Boston. Tituba's unplanned interaction with the medicine woman confirms the unity amongst the marginalized women. In Tituba's need, her progenitor, Mama Yaya sends Old Judah to guide Tituba as Mama Yaya fails to come personally. Additionally, Judah White enlightens Tituba by saying, "Men hate us, and yet without us their lives would be sad and narrow. […] we are the salt of the earth" (52). In Judah's words, men's lives are given meaning by women like Tituba, who enable them to shape their present and envision a better future. When Tituba feels helpless and clueless amidst the horror prevailing in Salem, Old Judah sends black cats as a gesture of her presence to accompany Tituba in her loneliness (66). Mama Yaya, Old Judah and Tituba are abhorred by society due to their link with the supernatural. However, they use magic to stay mutually related and resolve their challenges as a group.

A female black slave, Sarah, encourages Tituba to use her powers as a resistance against the whites to avenge the oppressed blacks. Joseph Henderson, Sarah's master, afflicts her with inhuman torture. The injury on Sarah's face and her "tiny hand, rough and rigid" (Condé 68) speaks for the cruelty of Joseph Henderson. Sarah's insufferable pain leads her to seek Tituba's aid to punish Joseph. Sarah persuades Tituba to use her magic against the white tormentors. Sarah says convincingly, "Knowledge must adapt itself to society […]. You [Tituba] are among monsters who are set on destroying us" (68). According to Sarah, Tituba should use her skills to protect her own people. However, Tituba needs to expand the functions of her knowledge to heal the oppressed and resist the monstrosity of the oppressors simultaneously. Sarah's words resonate with Tituba's "innermost thoughts" (68) as if Sarah had an indication from her ancestors. Sarah is not Tituba's friend, but having this conversation with Sarah instigates a desire for revenge in Tituba. Since Sarah and Tituba are both slaves enduring similar misfortunes, the urgency of Sarah's voice is better comprehended by Tituba. Consequently, Sarah's plea leaves Tituba in contemplation of a slave revolt in the future. Mama Yaya once instructed Tituba to use witchcraft only for healing and consoling her own people. However, Sarah arouses an interest in Tituba to use her artistry as a defence against the victimizers. Therefore, her conversation with Sarah stimulates Tituba to realize the necessity of using her powers to prevent the exploitation of the black slaves by their white masters.

Tituba's friendship with Hester guides her in eluding the death sentence in Salem Witch Trial and seeking revenge on her accusers by providing a false confession in court. Tituba meets Hester in prison. Hester is a black woman but not a slave like Tituba. Understanding their difference in social status, Tituba addresses Hester as her mistress. In response, Hester asks Tituba to call her by name (Condé 95). Hester's response to Tituba settles an equality between them. Later, Hester's remark on being an outcast like Tituba (96) indicates their equal share in misery as black women. Tituba learns that Hester's family "believed in sexual equality" (97) and taught her the classics. Nevertheless, Hester is imprisoned for committing adultery while "[…] the man who puts [his] child in [her] womb is free to come and go as he pleases" (97). Hester's husband participates in the same crime for which she is punished. Ironically, her husband is pardoned while she is convicted guilty. Listening to Hester makes Tituba realize that oppression is a collective experience for subjugated women. According to Young, "When women group, their womanliness [is not] the only thing that brings them together; there are other concrete details of their lives that give them affinity, such as their class or race position, their nationality, their neighbourhood, their religious affiliation" (737). Tituba's encounter with Hester enables her to realize the sufferings of all women as a whole, as she questions, "Are women condemned to such a fate in this world?" (Condé 98). Tituba's white mistress, Goodwife Parris, Hester, an educated black woman and Tituba herself as a black slave, are equally ill-fated. Furthermore, Hester influences Tituba to avenge herself by saying, "If some of them have wronged you in person, then take your revenge [...]" (100). Hester suggests Tituba not to be evil like her tormentors. However, she motivates Tituba to strike her accusers by providing a false confession that would also reduce Tituba's penalty. So, the alliance Tituba forms with Hester helps Tituba to dodge the death sentence that awaits her after the witch trial in Salem court.

After death, Tituba selects Samantha as her progeny to continue transgressing the span of abusive treatment of women that has been going on for generations. Tituba develops confidence and mental strength through bitter circumstances in her life. She returns to Barbados when the Jew, Benjamin Cohen d'Azevedo, discharges her from slavery. Acquiring freedom from enslavement and reuniting with her fellow people give Tituba a sense of belonging and hope. Shortly after returning to her native island, Tituba gets involved in a relationship with the leader of the maroons, Christopher. Tituba's newfound certainty enables her to cherish her pregnancy with Christopher's child. Referring to her previous pregnancy, Tituba writes, "For the first time I asked myself whether my child, whose life I had taken, would not, after all, have given my experience a meaning and a purpose" (Condé 152). It is apparent in Tituba's statement that she is no longer hesitant to have her child. Rather, she contemplates her child's ability to make her life significant and ambitious. Through her utterance, Tituba expresses her expectations for her offspring to salvage her heritage. Moreover, Tituba is determined to alter the destiny of the slaves as she does not want her descendant to suffer like she does. Tituba affirms, "No, if the world were going to receive my child, then it would have to change!" (159) because she refuses the victimization of her future generation by the whites. By claiming the world is unfit to receive her child, she denounces the stereotypes based on which black lives are incapacitated in the world. Tituba's future child functions as a driving force for her to try to resolve the discrimination and anticipate a habitable society for Black people. Later, Tituba devises a "general revolt" (161) against the planters with Iphigene, a boy whom she nurses back to health. Despite the "easily predictable" (166) downfall of their rebellion, Tituba is optimistic that her unborn daughter "would settle old scores" (167) for her. Unfortunately, Tituba is executed by the whites, and her biological daughter dies in the womb. However, the dead Tituba remains an inspiration amongst her people as she sustains her interaction with the living through her powers. Indicating other oppressed slaves, Tituba says, "I am nourishing them with dreams of liberty. ... I have been behind every revolt" (175). Additionally, Tituba singles out a curious girl named Samantha as her representative and prepares her for the journey ahead by disclosing "the hidden power of herbs" (177) to her since the initiative Tituba takes to disrupt the spiral of violence on the black women is required to be continued by Samantha as Tituba's progeny. Previously, when Tituba was young, Mama Yaya supported her to overcome the challenges as a black female slave. Likewise, Tituba dies as a revolutionary, but she ensures its continuation by sharing her ancestry with Samantha. Comprehending the cause of the present suffering of the blacks, Tituba anticipates, "I can understand the past, read the present, and look into the future. […] there will be an end to all this [suffering]. … What is one life in relation to the immensity of time?" (178). Noticeably, Mama Yaya is Tituba's connection to the past, while her present experiences enable her to acquire an insight into the upcoming future. Tituba concludes her story on an optimistic tone because the three generations of women – Mama Yaya, Tituba and Samantha – collaborate to liberate themselves and bring constructive changes in their lives.

Our analysis in this chapter attempts to prove that Condé's fictional Tituba's control of the novel's narrative allows her an expression that was denied to the historical Tituba by the colonial representation of Salem Witch Trial. We have also tried to show that the use of magic in the novel unites the women from three generations to defend their subordination as a team, while Tituba's friendship with other oppressed women contributes to her transformation. The magical realist narrative technique of *I,*

Tituba offers Tituba an agency to write her personal experiences in the novel. The historical Tituba's voice, which was suppressed by the documented reality, is provided with credibility through the expressions of the fictional Tituba. *I, Tituba* challenges the patriarchal representation of female experiences. Subsequently, Tituba uses her control over the novel's narrative to expose the injustice done to herself and other repressed female characters. As a result, Tituba's storytelling validates her personal expression from the perspective of a black female slave, contradicting the vague colonial portrayal of a slave's endurance. Moreover, Tituba demonstrates her victimization by her white mistress, Puritan master, black lovers and white children. So, her writing rejects male authority and reveals how she becomes an easy target of verbal insult, mental trauma and sexual abuse within the grasp of the men and white society. Through her narration, Tituba highlights the repugnance of the whites for the black slaves, driven by which they wrongfully accuse Tituba of being an evil 'witch' to persecute her. In other words, Tituba's story scrutinizes the discriminatory treatment she receives from the whites and indicates their failure to address a black slave woman's version of truth. Nevertheless, Tituba also describes the process of her change into a resilient individual amidst her sufferings. Initially, Tituba's writing offers her perspective as a victim. However, her voice acquires strength, confidence and deliverance as her story progresses. Tituba talks about the influence of Mama Yaya, Old Judah, Goodwife Parris, Sarah and Hester in her personal growth. In that regard, Tituba's description accentuates the contribution of other subjugated women, facilitating her transformation by offering her relief, guidance and motivation. In the next chapter, we will show that, like Tituba, the African American protagonist, Cocoa, from Gloria Naylor's *Mama Day,* struggles to overcome the obstacles of her life. Although Cocoa is not victimized by her male partner, she has different challenges to surpass. Cocoa shares an inseparable bond with her grandmothers, Miranda and Abigail, the same bond that Tituba shares with Mama Yaya and Abena. When Cocoa's life is threatened by Ruby's hoodoo, Miranda's magical power and Abigail's care facilitates her (Cocoa's) recovery.

| Chapter 3 |

Achieving Individual Transformation and Securing a Peaceful Future in Gloria Naylor's *Mama Day*

"They say every blessing hides a curse,
and every curse a blessing."

(Naylor 78)

In *Mama Day,* Gloria Naylor's heroine, Cocoa, an orphan black woman and a widow, undergoes a process of self-discovery through the life-altering phases of her life. Cocoa's conflict with the novel's villain, Ruby, threatens the harmony of her marriage. However, the process of her personal struggles solidifies her relationship with the matriarchs of her family, and she transforms into her best version. The inclusion of magical realism in *Mama Day* enables Cocoa's dead husband, George, to interact with her from his grave, creating a narrative that provides an insight into their marriage. The New York segment of the novel represents the rational world and describes both George and Cocoa's efforts to make necessary adjustments in their marriage as co-partners. Cocoa's relationship with George challenges a conventional marriage rooted in patriarchy. Unlike the patriarchal assumption, George is not a dominating husband but rather supports Cocoa in her individual interests. Therefore, Naylor's portrayal of George's character can be observed as a feminist expectation of a male partner. As Cocoa and George are equal partners in their marriage, Cocoa does not confront any patriarchal barrier to accomplish her goals. Cocoa's marital bond with George in *Mama Day* subverts patriarchy and gender stereotypes. We will concentrate on the mutual dependency between Cocoa and George to analyze his contribution to Cocoa's personal growth. On the other hand, Cocoa's life in Willow Springs concentrates mostly on her relationship with her grandmother, Abigail and great-aunt, Miranda. Cocoa is raised by them without a man's support. Miranda is a medicine woman who is addressed as 'Mama Day' in Willow Springs. Miranda is a dominant individual in the community as her superior knowledge exceeds science. Moreover, the magical realist elements of *Mama Day* become more pronounced when the novel's setting shifts to Willow Springs. The prevalent mysticism in the environment of Willow Springs links only the dominant women of the community. As a result, George's efforts to rescue Cocoa from Ruby's spell turn invalid as both Miranda's and Ruby's abilities overpower his. Later, Miranda's connection with the supernatural enables her to neutralize Ruby's hoodoo and save Cocoa's life. The female figures in Willow Springs appear more powerful than men to bear a greater impact on another woman's life. We will evaluate Cocoa's affinity with her grandmothers and her rivalry with Ruby to prove that jealousy among the women leads to a destructive outcome, whereas female solidarity offers a scope of healing and prosperity for them.

In *Mama Day,* Gloria Naylor delineates an ambitious heroine, Cocoa, who migrates to a foreign land to pursue her career. Cocoa is a resolute, confident and straightforward woman. Since the beginning of her courtship with George, Cocoa has been forthright regarding her expectations of him. After their marriage, Cocoa refuses to conceive a child and continues her higher education. So, Cocoa independently determines her identity and desires from life. Jones uses the term "Bulletproof Diva" to describe "A woman whose sense of dignity and self cannot be denied" (qtd in Springer 1072), and her definition fits Cocoa's characteristics. Consequently, it is likely that Cocoa marries George, envisioning the possibility of an egalitarian relationship with him. George's character challenges the male discourse, and unlike subservient wives, Cocoa executes equal authority over him. Susan Arndt claims that numerous African feminists strive to determine alternative opportunities for women to overcome their oppression by dismantling the patriarchal language and narrative technique (32-33). Additionally, Allison Drew states that African feminism attempts to "transform pre-existing gender relations to allow women and men equal rights and opportunities" (7) within a specific social context. Likewise, Naylor suspends patriarchal domination and violence to disrupt the traditional idea of marriage and provides Cocoa with an opportunity to thrive in her relationship with George.

In this chapter, we will argue that Cocoa's marital bond with George subverts the patriarchal depiction of a male partner, which epitomizes a positive and progressive male-female relationship. Despite George and Cocoa's strained initial interaction, they eventually develop a friendship that is beneficial for their maturation. Unlike most controlling and judgemental men, George values Cocoa's individual choices. As a result, George and Cocoa's reciprocal marriage enables Cocoa to concentrate on her personal growth after marriage instead of conforming to any patriarchal ideology. Moreover, the prevalent supernatural context of Willow Springs and the matriarchal Day family demonstrate female dominance. In Willow Springs, George serves more as a caregiver to Miranda, Abigail and Cocoa. Nevertheless, Cocoa's potential ally, Miranda, and the malevolent villain, Ruby, have more influence on Cocoa's life than George. George's logic and rationality fail to save Cocoa, whereas Miranda's mystic power restores Cocoa's health from Ruby's lethal spell. Therefore, the magical realism incorporated in *Mama Day* empowers the female characters to depict their impact on each other as a collective. Nesrin Yavaş talks about the use of magical realism in *Mama Day* to re-conceptualize the collective past to "empower black women through temporal and cultural changes" (253). Furthermore, Drew emphasizes the idea of female consciousness to formulate solidarity based on common experiences and oppression (8). As a result, the myth of Sapphira Wades' contribution to emancipating her predecessors, Miranda and Abigail, by resisting slavery in the past indirectly affects Cocoa's life. Miranda and Abigail witness the misfortune of the women born before Cocoa in the Day family. Their acknowledgement of the past misery solidifies their bond with Cocoa, and they consider securing a better future for her. In addition to Miranda's contribution in shaping the future of the women in Day family, she serves as a healer and Shaman in her community. Miranda's alliance with

Bernice indicates that she uses healing properties to aid the women of Willow Springs.

Correspondingly, we will argue that Cocoa's relationship with Abigail and Miranda functions as a catalyst in her maturation. We will evaluate Miranda's contribution to Cocoa's physical and emotional recovery to establish the significance of female friendship in empowering the afflicted women. Nevertheless, Kimberly Springer claims, "Competition, vying for status, and degraded self-worth can be Black women's worst interpersonal enemies" (1072). Indicating the failure of Black female solidarity, Morgan terms the envious women responsible for their own oppression as "Chickenheads" who disrupt the progress of the ambitious women (qtd in Springer 1073). Likewise, the insecure and malicious female character, Ruby, threatens Cocoa's marriage and her future. Although the malice spread by Ruby compromises George's life, Miranda's wisdom salvages Cocoa's future. In response to Ruby's aggression, Miranda retaliates and executes her superior knowledge to mutilate Ruby. On the other hand, Cocoa's long-suppressed insecurity and competition toward George's ex, Shawn, leads to an unhealthy outburst that nearly weakens the mutual respect between George and Cocoa. Therefore, the novel represents a vicious cycle of female rivalry. Nonetheless, we will draw a contrast between the catastrophic outcome of Ruby's jealousy towards Cocoa and the recuperative effect of Miranda's affinity in Cocoa's life. Hereafter, we will attempt to prove that Miranda, Abigail and Cocoa's relationship symbolizes the success of collective black sisterhood and confirms its ability to abolish female rivalry within the group.

Marriage is one of the patriarchal institutions. The prevalent male diction normalizes female subordination in marriage. It is typical for a woman to settle for a subservient position and sacrifice her individual accomplishments to concentrate on her domestic responsibilities. Atkinson talks about women's "psychological dilemma" to either resist oppression or accept their inferior position in marriage (104). Atkinson argues, "A woman's very life as a human being depends upon her attachment to, her identification with, her counterclass – men" (105). As a result, women instigate their own oppression by accepting male domination in marriage. However, Naylor subverts the patriarchal concept of marriage in *Mama Day* to suggest the possibility of mutual dependence between a man and a woman. In the novel, George and Cocoa are given equal control of the narrative to share their separate perspectives as well. Their marriage promotes mutuality as they compromise, adjust and evolve together to sustain a healthy bond. After marriage, Cocoa is not required to alter her lifestyle to match George's expectations. Rather, she continues focusing on her career and individual attainments. The absence of male authority in George enables Cocoa to secure her individuality after marriage. George discourages patriarchal values as he is sensible toward Cocoa's expectations of him. As a result, George's attributes attack the male stereotypes and alter the idea of marriage that can benefit female interests. During their courtship, George brings positive changes in Cocoa's life. In August 1999,

Cocoa revisits George's grave in Willow Springs. The magic realist elements present in the novel allow Cocoa to interact with George even after his death. Their non-verbal interaction retrospects their marital past and reveals its significance in Cocoa's life. Cocoa moves to New York to expand her possibilities. However, the new city makes Cocoa feel alienated, and she continuously struggles to adjust for seven years until she meets George through an interview. On their first date, George indicates that Cocoa is "shallow and a bigot" (Naylor 63) because she has a surface-level understanding of New York. George helps Cocoa to rediscover New York, enabling her to overcome her stereotypical treatment of the city. During one of their explorations in New York, Cocoa admits, "Standing there under and over all that incredible space, I saw how small and cramped my life had been" (98). George enables Cocoa to simultaneously acknowledge both Willow Springs' heritage and New York's culture, which broadens her perspective on how to thrive in the modern world. On the other hand, Cocoa and George's relationship is reciprocal. Cocoa influences George to become less arrogant and more giving. Roaming across New York with Cocoa reignites George's interest in this town, and Cocoa becomes more self-sufficient in his presence. Recalling the influence of their New York visits, George tells Cocoa, "You weren't becoming different, you were going back to the way you were. […] and I was so busy enjoying the change in you, I didn't notice it in myself" (100). After rediscovering New York with George for several days, Cocoa admits that he has already turned her into a better woman (104). Cocoa's remark confirms that she decides to marry George because he complements her.

George motivates Cocoa to inspect her flaws and exceed her previous self. During their courtship, George realizes that Cocoa is headstrong, insensitive, childish and irrational. Additionally, Cocoa is spontaneous and quick to give up whenever any situation goes beyond her control. However, George challenges Cocoa, tests her limits, and makes her work for what she wants. He denies Cocoa an immediate outcome and insists on her tolerance. Even Cocoa's letters to her great-aunt, Miranda, reveal that she finally meets a potential male partner. Appreciating George's arrival in Cocoa's life, Miranda says to Abigail, "She's [Cocoa] hard-headed, and she's spoiled, and this is one who won't let her have her way. I'm starting to like him already [...] it's gonna take a strong man to do her" (Naylor 109). According to Miranda, a sensible husband like George can guide Cocoa in correcting her mistakes for personal development. During the initial stage of their courtship, George simply ignores Cocoa's irrational demands as a constant assurance of his fondness for her. George refuses to provide Cocoa with a version of himself. She demands rather than insists that she accepts his actual self. Cocoa has an immature perception of a relationship and expects George to prioritize her over everything else in his life. George urges her to understand that his work, his health, and Monday nights are important to him. Initially, Cocoa tags George as "insensitive and selfish" (121) instead of accepting his individuality. Nevertheless, George's sensibility and persistence encourage Cocoa to respect their separate interests. Instead of asserting control over Cocoa,

George inspires Cocoa to understand his passion for football and consider the Monday nights for him. He avoids talking and cuddling with Cocoa to make her come to terms with his expectations (124). Eventually, Cocoa starts to complain less and understand George more through their attempt to create a balance in their relationship. Cocoa shares her personal life with George and unwillingly accepts his reluctance to do the same. Cocoa admits to George, "[…] since I refused to think of my life anymore without you in it, this was just the way it would have to be" (127). Cocoa's remark indicates that she is ready to accept the differences between George and her personality. Likewise, George eventually decides to express his own insecurities to Cocoa. So, George and Cocoa develop mutual understanding and respect to help each other improve at an individual level. George and Cocoa's courtship is sustained because of their willingness to compromise for each other. Additionally, George and Cocoa's attempt to make required adjustments promotes equality between them. George does not subordinate Cocoa but rather inspires her to evaluate her faults. As a result, Cocoa independently undergoes the process of self-exploration which benefits her interpersonal relationships in the future.

Unlike any typical marriage, George and Cocoa's relationship does not conform to the asymmetrical distribution of authority. While having a conversation with Miranda over the phone before marrying Cocoa, George tells her, "She [Cocoa] has all I have" (Naylor 136). After listening to George, Miranda is assured that he intends to share his life equally with Cocoa. Miranda explains

George's claim to Abigail by stating, "If he [George] got a life […] he's saying that life can open itself up for her. You can't ask for anything more than that from a man" (136). Miranda's statement reflects the expectations of a woman from her male partner. Cocoa and George's marriage shows the promise of compromising and sharing between them. Since George does not have a family, having a female partner "in itself was a challenge" for him (141). After marriage, ensuring Cocoa's comfort becomes George's priority. George purchases books to understand Cocoa's menstrual cycle and the reasons behind Cocoa's mood swings. Whenever Cocoa acts annoyed, George tries to figure out its cause, as his simple aspiration is to make Cocoa happy (142). George alters the patriarchal portrayal of a dominating and ill-treating husband.

According to Dreyer, "In male-dominated societies, women are socialized to accept negative images attributed to them by others […] and internalize this in the form of a negative self-perception which detracts from the possibility of having a meaningful life" (2). Contrarily to this patriarchal practice, George functions as a caregiver and asserts a sense of equivalency between Cocoa and himself. George tells Cocoa, "Living with a female: a day-to-day balancing act, and I really enjoyed the challenge. Because the times I got it right, your being different made all the difference in my world" (Naylor 143). In contrast to a patriarchal mindset, George aspires to be a supportive and compassionate husband to Cocoa. In recent days, an aspiring woman refuses to get married, contemplating the barriers she might face concerning her future goals. Robinson argues, "Marriage is rooted in a discourse of monogamy that privileges the interests of both men and capitalism, operating as it does through the mechanisms of exclusivity, possessiveness and jealousy" (144). Nevertheless, George's marriage with Cocoa portrays a standard male-female relationship that would interest an independent woman. It is observable that Cocoa is a self-sufficient woman whose life is not manipulated or determined by George. Cocoa's commitment to George facilitates her personal life, but she does not rely on George to shape her future. George shares the domestic chores with Cocoa so she gets sufficient time to focus on her own accomplishments. George earns sufficient money and does not require Cocoa's salary for financial support. However, Cocoa continues her job to assert her individuality. Furthermore, Cocoa refuses George's desire to start having children shortly after marriage and gets her history degree instead. This proves that Cocoa makes independent choices regarding her life and her career. When Cocoa quits her job, she tells her friends, "No, he [George] wasn't forcing me. I was hardly the type to be chained to a stove barefoot and pregnant. I'd be starting school in the fall" (Naylor 148). It is evident in Cocoa's statement that George's presence does not threaten her personal choices and individuality. The mutual dependency between George and Cocoa suggests a progressive relationship between them. During Thanksgiving, George prepares breakfast for Cocoa, and she spends the afternoon watching football with him before cooking dinner together (159). According to Miranda, George worships the ground Cocoa walks on (170). In other words, George is a facilitator in Cocoa's life, not her rescuer. As a result, George and Cocoa's relationship disassembles the patriarchal diction of a conventional marriage between a dependent female and a male subjugator.

After going to Willow Springs with Cocoa, George establishes a sense of unity with the matrons of the Day family. Commenting on Cocoa's grandmother, Abigail's affection for him, George states, "No woman had ever called me her child" (Naylor 176). George returns Miranda and Abigail's fondness for him with respect and gratitude. George's arrival makes Miranda happy, and she says, "It's good to have a man in the family again" (178). Her remark sheds light on the possibility of coexistence between men and women as long as it excludes patriarchal influence. This is contrary to the notion of "patriarchal terrorism", which Johnson defines as "a product of patriarchal traditions of men's right to control 'their' women, a form of terroristic control of wives by their husbands that involves the systematic use of not only violence, but economic subordination, threats, isolation, and other control tactics" (284). Miranda observes that George is kind and compassionate, unlike the typical men. Therefore, any other man but George would have failed to convert Cocoa into her best version. Miranda says, "A woman shouldn't have to fight her man to be what she was: he should be fighting that battle for her" (Naylor 203). According to Miranda, a woman's relationship with a man should not compromise her actual self; rather, he is expected to expedite her individuality. She notices the potential in George to complement Cocoa. Nevertheless, Miranda admits that men were more stereotypical during her time, and George is a rare exception in the present. That being the case, many young women decide to stay unmarried and alone as claimed by Miranda (203). Her comment does not promote misandry. However, it can be evaluated as a resistance against the patriarchal notions that create a conflict in a heterosexual relationship. George's rejection of male stereotypes enables him to form a friendship with Miranda and Abigail. George offers Miranda and Abigail domestic help. He paints the house, fixes the garden, cleans Miranda's rugs, and willingly performs other household chores to aid the matriarchs. In response, Abigail feeds him peanuts, and Miranda massages his aching shoulders after a tiring day. Commenting on Miranda and Abigail's control over George, Cocoa tells him, "They had you under their heels, and you were purring" (217). Cocoa's statement highlights the feminine qualities in George's character, which transcend the gender binary. His sensitivity allows him to become a component of the sorority that Miranda, Abigail and Cocoa share.

George intends to protect Cocoa in any situation that threatens her well-being. When Ruby's spell endangers Cocoa's life, George attempts everything within his capability to relieve her. Even Miranda realizes that she requires George's assistance along with her magic, "So [that] together they could be the bridge for Baby Girl [Cocoa] to walk over" (Naylor 285). Her contemplation confirms that Miranda is required to guide George to ensure success, as he alone cannot restore Cocoa's health. According to Tucker, "[…] Miranda depends on George's belief in himself, his ability to work with his hands, his resolve to hold on to what he loves, to never let Cocoa go" (182). Miranda's desire to cooperate with George accentuates the necessity of mutual dependency between men and women. Miranda and George's joint efforts are crucial for Cocoa's recovery because George's belief in Miranda's connection with the supernatural can facilitate the completion of Miranda's healing ritual. Miranda instructs George to bring whatever he finds inside the nest of the biggest chicken in her coop and join her along with it in the "other place" (Naylor 295). However, George depicts the task as "mumbo-jumbo" (295) and refuses to trust Miranda's capabilities. Despite his inability to comprehend Miranda's instructions, George performs the task in his desperation to save Cocoa. Unfortunately, his reluctance to act in unison with Miranda leads to his failure to protect Cocoa. Nonetheless, George's selfless act to aid Cocoa alters the gender hegemony. As stated by Cowart, "Naylor proposes a radically feminist revision of traditional patriarchal narrative. In *Mama Day*, she implies that humanity will achieve its redemption only by restoring the proper mythic/religious relations between the sexes" (64). George inspires Cocoa to be considerate and rational during their four years of marriage. During his stay in Willow Springs, he builds an attachment with Miranda and Abigail. Later, George fails to execute Miranda's instructions but his willingness to act in unison with Miranda confirms the mutual dependency between them. This competent relationship between George, Cocoa, Miranda, and Abigail challenges the tendency of patriarchal society to determine men as dominant and women as submissive. After George's death, Cocoa marries a man who is respectful towards her choices. Cocoa's second husband does not object when she names her youngest boy after George. Similarly, he does not complain when Cocoa visits George's grave. As a result, Cocoa's selection of supportive individuals further confirms the kind of amity she desires from her male partner. Therefore, Cocoa's relationship with George denotes a criticism of patriarchal values and offers an alternative male-female relationship that resonates with feminine interests.

Miranda can efficiently assist Cocoa while she stays amidst the mysticism of Willow Springs, but Cocoa's life in the rational world is mainly guided by George. The myth of Sapphira Wade, the unreal atmosphere, and the powerful female shamans provide Willow Springs with a spiritual quality. The magic realist setting of Willow Springs allows the medicine women authority over the men in the community. According to Bowers, when magic realism is perceived "from the position of the 'other' and is considered to bring into view non-logical and non-scientific explanations for things, [then] …the transgressive power of magical realism provides a means to attack the assumptions of the dominant culture and particularly the notion of scientifically and logically determined truth" (65). So, the matriarchs of the Day family challenge male domination by asserting their control over George. Additionally, Miranda's ability to salvage Cocoa despite George's non-performance accentuates her contribution to Cocoa's retrieval. Based on the folklore, Miranda and Abigail's ancestor, Sapphira Wade, resists slavery and ensures a better future for her progenies. According to Miranda's father, John-Paul, the candle walk was performed in Sapphira Wade's memory of resistance during his time (Naylor 111). The history of the Day family glorifies female authority and its influence in liberating the community from slavery. Sapphira Wade reformulates the future of her female descendants, Miranda and Abigail, allowing them an agency to live a dignified life. Consequently, Miranda and Abigail's guidance empowers Cocoa to cross the boundary of Willow Springs and thrive in the modern world. Furthermore, Cocoa's grandmothers function as a constant aid in her individual development. As a result, the Day family women demonstrate a strong sense of solidarity, highlighting its importance in women's emancipation.

Miranda's wisdom permits her to guide her grandniece, Cocoa, whom she raised "like her very own" (Naylor 9). Miranda descends directly from Sapphira Wade. Miranda's connection with the supernatural gives her an authoritative position in the community. Both men and women of Willow Springs obey her in a way that if "Mama Day says no, everybody says no" (6). Miranda and Abigail raise Cocoa with the utmost sensibility because Cocoa is their ultimate hope. Yavaş claims, "Being 'the last of the womenfolk come into the Days,' Cocoa's survival is paramount to the active reconstruction and rehistoricizing of black women's history […]" (252). As a result, Miranda and Abigail monitor and mould Cocoa's personality since her childhood. Thereupon, Cocoa grows into a confident individual who is capable of determining her self-sufficiency. Despite her physical presence, Miranda confirms Cocoa's sustenance in the New York environment. When Cocoa returns home, instead of joining George's firm, Miranda urges Cocoa to write a letter to George, informing her interest in taking the position. Later,

Miranda mails the letter on Cocoa's behalf after sprinkling some mysterious powder inside the envelope. The scent of lavender from the powder enlivens George's memory of Cocoa. Before receiving the letter, George was discouraged from reconnecting with Cocoa. Nonetheless, the mysterious powder reminds George of Cocoa, and he remarks, "As the water ran and the powder finally dissolved from my fingers, it all came back, a movie being played in reverse frame to frame [...] your [Cocoa's] neck. There was now the faintest scent of lavender on my wet fingers [...]" (Naylor 54). It is evident that Miranda's magic intervenes to secure Cocoa's job. Moreover, the mystic connection he felt during his brief encounter with Cocoa at the coffee shop resurfaces after Cocoa's letter to George. As a result, Miranda exhibits her efficiency in manipulating Cocoa's life by performing as a guide and mediator.

Miranda and Abigail's co-parenting can be evaluated as a form of sisterhood among women. Miranda disciplines Cocoa to foster a sense of responsibility in her. On the other hand, Cocoa's grandmother, Abigail, reduces Cocoa's frustration by offering comfort through her warmth and affection. Unlike Abigail's tenderness, Miranda strictly regulates Cocoa's actions to improve her personality. Cocoa admits that Abigail alone would have failed to raise her properly. Miranda and Abigail together shape Cocoa into a qualified woman. Cocoa states, "It seemed I could do no wrong with her [Abigail], while with Mama Day I could do no right [...] together they were the perfect mother" (Naylor 58). Abigail's undivided compassion for Cocoa permits Miranda to enforce discipline without suffocating her grandniece. Likewise,

Abigail's tolerance for Cocoa's tantrums offers her a space to live carefree within a limit. Furthermore, Abigail serves as a peacemaker whenever Miranda and Cocoa's bond is strained. After a year of her marriage with George, Cocoa visits Willow Springs and fights with Miranda because she discourages Cocoa from going beyond the bridge to watch Muddy Waters play. During the fight, Cocoa becomes agitated and addresses Miranda as "an overbearing and domineering old woman" (156). Later, Abigail tries to convince Miranda that "She [Cocoa] ain't meant it" (157) to mitigate the tension between Miranda and Cocoa. The exchange of acknowledgement and affinity between Cocoa and her grandmothers takes the shape of female friendship. Referring to her attachment with Miranda and Abigail, Cocoa says, "[...] even if hate and rage were to tear us totally apart, they knew I was always theirs" (177), which indicates the presence of an inseparable bond between them. Additionally, Miranda contributes to sustaining a healthy marriage of her grandniece. After Cocoa's worst fight with George, Miranda advises her to forgive him by stating, "[...] if you care about someone enough, you give 'em a chance to take back the things they may have said in anger" (240). Later, Abigail reveals her "no-nonsense, clinical efficiency" (260) when Cocoa's life is threatened by Ruby. In George's words, Abigail is doing everything within her capability in the absence of a doctor to restore Cocoa's health (260). Similarly, Miranda interacts with the supernatural to Cocoa's advantage. Therefore, Miranda and Abigail's relationship with Cocoa benefits her in every phase of her life.

Miranda is an indigenous medicine woman in Willow Springs, a territory detached from the outside world. Miranda and Abigail's knowledge of herbal remedies provides them with an agency to help people. Subsequently, Miranda is more reliable than a doctor in her community. Miranda utilizes the healing properties of herbs to restore the health of a woman, Bernice. In her desperation to get pregnant, Bernice infects her ovaries by consuming unnecessary fertility pills without medical advice. However, Bernice can still have a baby after recovering from the infection because she has been taking herbal tea prepared by Miranda (Naylor 87). Miranda's concern for Bernice's well-being seals their unity. On the contrary, Miranda's adversarial relationship with her neighbour, Ruby, disrupts the concept of sorority among women. Unlike Miranda, Ruby practices hoodoo to execute her evil intentions. Ruby's curse on Cocoa initiates a rivalry with the Day family. Ruby intends to sabotage Cocoa and George's marriage because she is envious of Cocoa's healthy marriage. Ruby's desperation to diminish Cocoa's personal progress leads to a devastating outcome in both Cocoa and her life. The aftermath of Ruby's antagonism criticizes the conflict among women and its liability to hinder their emancipation as a collective.

Ruby's unhealthy competition with both Cocoa and Frances disrupts their individual potential. Ruby's toxic relationship with Junior Lee and her personal failures turn her malevolent. Her husband, Lee, marries Ruby for her wealth. Ruby sabotages Lee's previous relationship with Miss Frances to redirect his interest in herself. Frances complains to Miranda that Ruby is messing with Junior

Lee's mind by mixing potions in his food (Naylor 90). Presumably, Ruby murders her first husband because he cheats on her. Likewise, her second husband, Lee, is a drunk who gambles and frequently visits prostitutes (69). Ruby has a history of failed marriages, which explains her tendency to sabotage another woman's life. Mavin and Grandy term this tendency of female rivalry as "Queen Bee Syndrome," stating, "The Queen Bee is commonly constructed as a 'bitch' who stings other women if her power is threatened" (224). In her desperation to possess Junior Lee, Ruby corrupts Frances' sanity as she ignores Ruby's warning to maintain her distance from him. During one of her visits to Willow Springs after marriage, Cocoa decides to spend her Saturday night beyond the bridge where Lee is also going. Ruby feels insecure and decides to get rid of Cocoa. Miranda senses Ruby inching across the woods, collecting castor beans, nightshade, and snakeroot to devise a new spell suitable for her evildoing. Sensing Ruby's jealousy, Miranda warns her, "Ain't a hoodoo anywhere as powerful as hate. Don't make me tangle with you […]" (Naylor 157). As a result, Ruby's intention to harm Cocoa provokes an enmity with Miranda. Nonetheless, "What goes around comes around" (162), and Ruby starts facing the consequences of her deeds. At night, Junior Lee sneaks out of the house and drives beyond the bridge to meet an anonymous woman. Ruby's magic cannot reach that far, so she can only wonder and lose her mind. Noticeably, she faces the same misery that she causes in Frances' life. Ruby's inability to appreciate another woman instigates malice in Frances, Miranda, Cocoa, and her own life. The people of Willow Springs fear and despise

Ruby for her envious nature. However, Ruby continues committing evil, which upsets the peacefulness of Cocoa's marital life with George.

In *Mama Day*, Naylor brings Ruby as a female antagonist to show the catastrophic outcome of jealousy among women. In contrast, the intimate bond between Cocoa, Miranda, and Abigail acts as a vibrant example of the rejuvenating aspects of female friendship. Ruby's rivalry with Cocoa and Miranda begins to take shape when Cocoa visits Willow Springs with George. After Cocoa and George's arrival, Ruby interrupts the Day family dinner by coming to meet George along with her husband, Lee. Ruby tells George, "You're one of us, 'cause you married one of us. And Cocoa is our own" (181). Apparently, Ruby's words are pretentious because she is not a well-wisher of Cocoa. Contrarily, Ruby envies Cocoa because she has everything that Ruby can possibly wish for: an independent identity and a caring husband. Unlike Lee, George is successful in his individual accomplishments and complements Cocoa as a husband. Ruby's denial to let Cocoa continue a better life than her leads to devastating consequences. Ruby casts hoodoo to create tension in Cocoa's marriage. As a result, Cocoa starts acting bluntly, which triggers frequent fights with George. Eventually, Miranda starts sensing death everywhere, which indicates that an imminent danger is about to threaten a member of the Day family (226). Later, Ruby catches Junior Lee flirting with Cocoa. Although Cocoa is not least flattered by Lee's attempt, it provides Ruby with a strong motif to sabotage Cocoa's healthy marriage. The absence of mutual understanding between Ruby and Cocoa creates hostility between them. Ruby pretends to be empathetic and invites Cocoa to her house. Ruby massages an unknown solution into Cocoa's scalp, makes tight braids and asks Cocoa to burn the loose hairs after returning home (246). Ruby's bizarre act hints at the dark ritual she intends to perform. Consequently, Cocoa's health deteriorates after meeting Ruby. Everything around Cocoa starts feeling like "A whirl of confusing echoes – visual, emotional, verbal" (259) to her. Cocoa's declining physical state is the result of Ruby's contempt for Cocoa. On the other hand, Cocoa expresses similar hatred for George's previous lover, Shawn, during her worst fight with him. Cocoa addresses Shawn as "your [George] precious redhead with freckles" (234) to provoke a fight with George. Cocoa's envy towards Shawn reflects on her self-doubt. The tension between Cocoa and Shawn challenges Cocoa's marriage as she hits George's head with a vase to release her frustration. So, George and Cocoa's fight can be observed as the unpleasant outcome of Cocoa's insecurity. Similarly, Ruby is finally held accountable for her actions. Miranda reveals her intention to punish Ruby by saying, "You play with people's lives, and it backfires on you" (261). Her statement suggests that every act of hatred misfires and causes equal damage to the attacker. Therefore, her claim criticizes female rivalry.

George's death and Miranda's revenge on Ruby validate the popular phrase, 'as the call, so the echo'. Ruby's curse on Cocoa endangers her life. In response to the damage that Ruby causes in Cocoa's life, Miranda denies Ruby a chance to redeem herself. Miranda sprinkles some enchanted powder around Ruby's house while she is hiding inside. Subsequently, a thunder explodes Ruby's house twice, destroying her wealth and fatally burning her. Observing the way Ruby's own deeds retaliates, George comments, "It seemed that she'd had a host of sins, going back several years, so the destruction of everything she owned and the burns on her body was her getting her due" (Naylor 274). Ruby is punished, but the course of her spell is irreversible. Miranda's supernatural abilities rescue Cocoa. Nonetheless, George's life is compromised in the process. As a result, George's death symbolizes the extreme outcome of female jealousy. Evidently, Ruby is responsible for her own downfall as she misuses her power to threaten the lives of other women. As the upshot of the ongoing exchange of contempt among women, Frances loses her sanity, Miranda mutilates Ruby, and Cocoa suffers a personal loss. Meanwhile, the consensus shared by Cocoa, Miranda, and Abigail reinstates the vitality of Cocoa's future. Miranda encourages George to assist her in Cocoa's recovery as "[...] she recognizes his strength and seeks to convert it to her ends. That is, she asks him, in the name of his love for Cocoa, to suspend his scepticism and serve her" (Cowart 71). Likewise, when George acts sceptical of Miranda and Abigail's capability to reclaim Cocoa's wellness, Cocoa expresses her faith in her grandmothers and tells George, "[...] these were the women who raised me – I would trust them with my life, and so whatever Mama Day had done, it was for a good reason" (Naylor 273). Subsequently, it is Miranda, Abigail, and Cocoa's shared empathy and togetherness that expedite Cocoa's recovery. Later, Miranda and Abigail's endurance enables Cocoa to self-actualize after George's death. Thus, Miranda,

Abigail, and Cocoa's relationship restores the continuity of female solidarity that Ruby attempts to jeopardize.

Miranda, Abigail, and Cocoa's relationship evolves when Ruby uses her powers to disrupt the harmony of the Day family. Miranda and Abigail spend sleepless nights to nurse Cocoa during her sickness. The shared sense of sisterhood between Miranda and Abigail again serves its usefulness to ease Cocoa's sufferings. Abigail relentlessly monitors Cocoa at home while Miranda frequents the other place to devise a cure for Cocoa. Observing the "[…] slump in Abigail's shoulders and the dark circles under her eyes" (Naylor 264), Miranda prepares herbal tea to withdraw Abigail's tiredness. On the other hand, Miranda untwists Cocoa's braids, cleans the poison infecting her scalp, and applies an ointment over it. Miranda is willing to sacrifice her own life if it ensures Cocoa's recovery. Miranda and Abigail fight for Cocoa's life when she belongs to them. After marriage, Cocoa is George's responsibility. Nonetheless, Miranda is willing to fight for Cocoa again and sacrifice her life if required (265). Apparently, Miranda and Abigail intend to protect Cocoa in every phase of her life. After George's death, Cocoa starts to believe that her life ends with him and considers committing suicide. However, Miranda offers Cocoa a reason to rebuild her life. Referring to George's death, Miranda tells Cocoa, "There ain't no pain – no pain – that you could be having worse than what that boy went through for your life" (302). So, Miranda encourages Cocoa to regain confidence in herself and shape her future in George's absence. After returning to New York, Cocoa finds it impossible to accept the disrupted order of her house, and Miranda urges Cocoa to deal with her trauma instead of wasting her time crying. Nevertheless, Miranda avoids comforting Cocoa because crying is a natural process of grieving. Instead, she waits for Cocoa to stop lamenting for herself someday. According to Miranda, "She's [Cocoa] gotta get past the grieving for what she lost" (308) to overcome her misfortune and re-establish hope for her future. Miranda's guidance enables her to mature and compensate for her personal loss. Thereupon, Cocoa's grandmothers teach Cocoa to meditate on tolerance, which aids her emotional recovery. Eventually, Cocoa's grief subsides, and she moves to Charleston to support her self-exploration. Her second marriage indicates that she accepts the past loss and considers reshaping her life with whatever good that the present offers her. Furthermore, Cocoa stops evading George's memory, considers preserving it, and starts visiting George's grave to sustain her connection with him. It is apparent that Miranda and Abigail's presence in Cocoa's life ensures her physical and emotional recovery from Ruby's aggression. Additionally, the struggle to reformulate Cocoa's future strengthens the bond between Miranda, Abigail, and Cocoa. For this reason, their integrity challenges the continuance of hatred among women. At the end of the novel, Miranda says, "Some things change [...] some things are yet to be" (312). Her observation indicates that human life is not linear, and our actions determine the change in the present, consequently affecting the future. Likewise, uprightness among women can eradicate the possibility of conflict. Furthermore, the mutual understanding can solidify their bond to facilitate their individual identity formation, hastening their advancement as a collective.

In this chapter, we have attempted to prove that Cocoa's marriage with George adds additional benefits to her personal growth as George challenges the exploitative treatment of men towards women. Thereby, the portrayal of his character reflects the feminist expectations from male partners to promote equality and individuality in marriage. Four years of marriage teaches Cocoa acceptance and compromise. Both George and Cocoa make adjustments to secure their separate identities after marriage. George does not limit Cocoa's personal ambitions but rather supports her in continuing higher education. Likewise, when Cocoa decides to keep her job, George shares the household chores to ease Cocoa's workload. Later, George befriends Miranda and Abigail during his visit to Willow Springs. He aids the Day family women whenever his assistance is expected from them. In the end, George tries everything in his capability until his death to ensure Cocoa's treatment. Hence, George rejects the patriarchal values and promotes Cocoa's individual identity formation. Additionally, we have demonstrated the importance of Cocoa's mutual attachment to Miranda and Abigail in reconstructing her future. Due to Miranda and Abigail's proper upbringing, Cocoa develops a resolute and confident personality. They support Cocoa to survive in the challenging environment of New York for seven years before George's arrival. Similarly, Miranda facilitates Cocoa's relationship with George as a mediator and a guide. When Cocoa is fatally inflicted by Ruby's curse, Abigail persistently nurses Cocoa while Miranda performs supernatural rituals to restore

Cocoa's health. Abigail and Miranda's unyielding affection for Cocoa terminates Ruby's hoodoo and reclaims her life. Moreover, they offer Cocoa emotional support to recover from her trauma after George's death. As a result, Miranda, Abigail, and Cocoa's integration formulates a support system for Cocoa's empowerment.

We have analyzed Miranda's resistance against the devastating result of Ruby's antagonism towards Cocoa and showed the efficiency of the female support system in preventing intragroup conflict. Ruby competes with Cocoa because her husband, Junior Lee, flirts with her. The devastating outcome of Ruby's spell takes George's life and nearly sabotages Cocoa's future. Nonetheless, Miranda avenges Cocoa by condemning Ruby for her evil deeds and brings stability in Cocoa's life. As a result, Miranda and Abigail's inclination to guard Cocoa from Ruby's hostility confirms the significance of female friendship in aiding a victimized woman. This chapter establishes the influence of Miranda and Abigail to foster the self-empowerment of Cocoa, an African-American heroine. Female friendship allows Naylor's protagonist to find solace in the most difficult phases of her life, while the incorporation of magic realism within the narrative allows her to connect with her beloved even after his death. In the next chapter of the book, we will critically assess the elements that promote the self-actualization of another black female protagonist, Celie, in *The Color Purple*. Unlike Cocoa, Celie initially lacks ambitions to secure her individuality and gets mutilated by black men. Luckily, the black women in Celie's life offer her support and motivation to resist male oppression. Just like Cocoa's relationship with Miranda and Abigail, Celie's shared sisterhood with other black women offers her comfort and guidance to rehabilitate her (Celie's) future. We will analyze the mutual relationship between the black female characters in *The Color Purple* to demonstrate how it promotes and expedites their liberation.

| Chapter 4 |

Female Friendship and Rejection of Male Supremacy in Alice Walker's *The Color Purple*

"[...] I see and hear you clearly, Great Mystery, now that I expect to see and hear you everywhere I am, which is the right place."

(Walker 10)

In the preface of her novel, *The Color Purple,* Alice Walker talks about her Black-American heroine, Celie's "rebirth into strong feelings of Oneness" (10), which offers Celie an opportunity to reclaim her individuality. The novel begins with Celie's letter to God that reveals her victimization by her adoptive father, Alphonso. He limits Celie's free existence and forces her into an incestuous relationship with him. Moreover, Celie's misfortune leads her to an unhappy marriage with her husband, Albert, who is mostly addressed as 'Mr. ___' in the novel. Albert treats Celie as an object, replicating Alphonso's attitude towards her. Both Alphonso and Albert exploit Celie's vulnerability and demand her conformity to their unfair treatment. As a result, Celie lacks self-efficacy and seeks temporary relief in her letters to God.

On the other hand, Celie's friendship with the women contradicts her relationship with the men. Celie's interpersonal relationships with Shug, Nettie, Sofia, and Mary Agnes allow Celie a safe space to recover from men's hostility and inspect her inaction. Celie, Shug, Nettie, Sofia, and Mary Agnes can relate to their personal misery; hence, they develop mutual concern for one another.

In *The Color Purple,* Celie is initially depicted as a sufferer who manifests an abundance of prosperity in her life by embracing her inner spirit at last. Noticeably, Celie writes her first letter to God as a victim, whereas she expresses her gratitude to "Dear Everything" (259) in her concluding letter as a reformed individual. Eventually, Celie asserts her individual identity, becomes financially self-sufficient, regains the ownership of her parental home, and reconnects with her lost sister, Nettie. However, the reconstruction of Celie's future is a controlled process, influenced by her personal awareness and interaction with individuals.

The Color Purple starts with Celie's letter to God, quoting the warning of her adoptive father, Alphonso. In the first line of the novel, Celie writes, *"You better not never tell nobody but God. It'd kill your mammy"* (3). Evidently, Alphonso asks Celie to stay silent regarding his evildoing unless she wants her mother tortured to death. His admonition to prevent Celie from publicly disclosing her physical exploitation by him indicates the extreme state of Celie's victimization through patriarchal agency. Celie's letters to God can be observed as her desire to escape her trauma by telling her unfortunate experiences to a listener. Alice Walker coined the term "womanism", which aims to "speak to all women and especially to black women" (Nfah-Abbenyi 122). In this regard, Nfah-Abbenyi writes about the black female writers who "seek to 'subvert and demythologize indigenous male writings and traditions which seek to label [them]'" (117). Correspondingly, Celie's letters written to God and especially to her sister, Nettie, serve as her reaction to male subjugation, indicating her attempt to create a space for self-expression. In the novel, the black female characters use a comic tone every so often to address the male characters. Observing Harpo's lack of presumed masculinity, Celie identifies him as "weak in will" and "scared" (Walker 28). Later, Shug labels Celie's husband, Albert, as a "weak little boy" (45) to attack his so-called manliness. Moreover, Celie remarks on a man's resemblance to a frog to insult Albert indirectly (230). Gloria Kaufman writes, "*Female* humor may ridicule a person or a system from an accepting point of view [...] while the *nonacceptance* of oppression characterizes feminist humor and satire" (13). Accordingly, Rebecca Krefting writes about the "Jokesters" who seek to "unmask inequality", pinpoint the stereotypical social norms responsible for the marginalization of a group, destabilize the standardized beliefs by "joking about them", and "[offer] new solutions and strategies" (2). As a result, Celie and Shug's mocking tone can be observed as one of the tools used to subvert typical masculine traits. Additionally, Celie seeks compassion and understanding in her romantic involvement with Shug, as Celie's marriage with Albert lacks these. Celie senses emotional and physical attraction towards Shug, which she does not feel for any man. On the other hand, Shug defines Celie as a "virgin" (Walker 74) after learning about Celie's unsentimental marriage with Albert and helps Celie explore her sexuality. Eventually, Shug and Celie develop a homosexual relationship between them. Ti-Grace Atkinson writes, "[Lesbianism] is the association by choice of individual members of any oppressed group – the massing of power – which is essential to resistance" (132). Therefore, Celie's homosexuality indicates her denial to stay with a man. In this chapter, I will argue that the feminist satire and homosexual reference incorporated in the novel delineate women's revulsion against the mortifying upshot of male supremacy. Celie's detest for men makes her feel comfortable only around women. So, she develops a friendship with Sofia, Shug, and Mary Agnes. Celie's exchange of letters with Nettie and her reciprocal relationship with the black women allow her an opportunity to deny subjugation. Jennifer Hamer and Helen Neville write about black women's need to "reach consensus" regarding the factors that sustain their inferiority to ensure change and a continuing integration among themselves (23). Black women need to acknowledge the source of their victimization before they can unify and reformulate their lives. The black female characters in the novel are vulnerable to the same prejudicial norms that threaten their individuality. Subsequently, they form a sisterhood based on support and empathy. An alliance can be developed among women who group together to renounce men (Atkinson 136). So, Celie, Sofia, Nettie, Mary Agnes, and Shug's common goal is to transcend the patriarchal barriers, which take the shape of black female unity. We shall prove that the corresponding friendship between Celie, Shug, Sofia, Nettie, and Mary Agnes implies the necessity of the black women's collaborative effort to accomplish their shared desire for emancipation, as they cannot ensure that separately. Celie's interaction with other female characters allows her relief from an unhappy and abusive marriage. However, Celie's maturation is supported by self-help as well. Noticeably, Sofia, Nettie, and Shug are already assertive enough to make an effort to improve their personal lives. Contrarily, Celie and Mary Agnes lack adequate motivation to alter their misfortune. Nonetheless, they get inspired by Sofia, Nettie, and Shug to initiate their personal growth. Initially, Celie ignores the suggestions that she receives from Nettie and Albert's sister, Kate, to resist domestic violence. Celie disregards Nettie's advice by confessing that she only knows how to survive (Walker 18). Similarly, Celie expresses her submissiveness in response to Kate's instruction, saying, "I don't fight, I stay where I'm told. But I'm alive" (22). Robin S. Dillon writes, "Deep and enduring shame and self-contempt, unremitting doubts about one's worth [...] such things constrict and deform lives, frustrating the quest for self-fulfillment and self-realization" (52). As a result, male diction and stereotypical norms corrupt women's idea of self-worth to sustain their victimization. Correspondingly, Celie is misguided by Albert and Alphonso's derogatory treatment and yields to their control as she lacks self-validation. The black women in Celie's life inspire her to fight for herself. Nevertheless, Celie's attempt to challenge her objectification involves her willingness and active participation to conquer her passivity. Dillon observes that "self is worthy of respect, [and] deserves attention [of] one's own" (60). Therefore, "[self-respect] encourages us to take seriously our complexity and fragmentation" and to realize the necessity of "self-construction" (Dillon 60). We shall argue that Celie's personal efforts to reclaim her selfhood enable her to resist male authority, reformulate her self-image, and secure her future. Alongside Celie's friendship with the black women, her self-help to recognize her worth equally contributes to the rehabilitation of her inner strength.

Celie starts facing male violence from an early age. Celie is only fourteen years old when her adoptive father, Alphonso, begins assaulting her. Demonstrating Alphonso's cruelty to her, Celie states, "He never had a kind word to say to me" (Walker 3). When Celie's mother falls ill, Alphonso rapes Celie and compels her to stay silent and get accustomed to his aggression (3). Unfortunately, Celie is impregnated by Alphonso, and Celie's mother dies yelling and cursing her for the unintended pregnancy. Despite that, Celie has to conceal Alphonso's identity when Celie's mother urges her to reveal the father of her illegitimate child (4). Celie's restrained expression reflects the terror that Alphonso provokes in her. Alphonso sabotages Celie's relationship with her mother by suppressing Celie's voice. As a result, both Celie and her mother are the victims of Alphonso's exploitative treatment and ignorance. Moreover, Alphonso murders Celie's first child, the product of his rape (4). Annoyed by Celie's second pregnancy, Alphonso labels Celie as an "evil" who is "always up to no good" (5). Consequently, he sells Celie's little boy, intending to get rid of his unwanted baby. Apparently, Alphonso denies Celie her sexual and reproductive choices. Alphonso treats Celie like a sexual object. Una Stannard mocks, "[…] food and women should become interchangeable commodities and sexual equivalents […] The food she serves is herself, and she, like the food, wants to be swallowed by the man [...]" (qtd. in Kaufman and Blakely 170-171). Correspondingly, Celie's unwilling, incestuous relationship with Alphonso consumes her. Besides, Alphonso beats Celie to control her, and she admits that her mother's downfall is also an outcome of his stereotypical values. Celie relates to her mother's misery and concedes, "I felt sorry for mama. Trying to believe his [Alphonso] story kilts her" (Walker 7). Additionally, Alphonso denies Celie proper schooling as he intends to subjugate her and limit her life within the household's margin. When Albert approaches Alphonso to seek Nettie's hand in marriage, Alphonso persuades him to marry Celie instead. Noticeably, Alphonso can no longer tolerate Celie and targets Nettie to exploit next. So, he tries to convince Albert to choose Celie and tells him, "She [Celie] ain't fresh tho, but I specs you know that. She spoiled. Twice" (9). Alphonso's comment echoes Sheila Ballantyne's character, the primitive man, who says after his wife's childbirth, "I just can't stand her no more! She lie there alla time havin babies, got no use for me" (qtd. in Kaufman and Blakely 161). Ironically, Alphonso rapes Celie, and it is discriminatory to identify her as 'evil' and 'spoiled'. However, Alphonso uses these terms to derogate Celie's identity. Furthermore, Alphonso threatens Celie's individuality by manipulating Albert's perception of her. Alphonso demeans Celie's identity while trying to convince Albert to marry her. In Alphonso's words, "[...] I got to git rid of her [...] She ugly [...] She ain't smart either [...] But she can work like a man" (Walker 10). Evidently, Alphonso observes Celie as an object and exploits her human identity. Likewise, based on his choice of words, it is observable that

Celie is given in marriage more as a domestic help than as a wife. According to Alphonso, Celie matches the qualities of a presumed good wife, as her lack of intelligence makes her vulnerable to Albert's dominance. Alphonso represents the male prejudices that impede Celie's personal growth. Thereupon, Celie's letters to God criticize patriarchal values and invigorate her defiance against male subjugation.

Celie's husband, Albert, is another representative of a stereotypical male. Comparing Albert to Alphonso, Celie says, "My little sister Nettie is got a boyfriend [Albert] in the same shape almost as Pa [Alphonso]" (Walker 6). Albert's initial decision was to marry Nettie, and it took him an entire spring to consider Celie instead (11). Alphonso puts Celie on display for Albert "Like it wasn't nothing" (12) when Albert desires another glance at her before marriage. So, Celie is treated like a product by these two vicious men. Observing Celie's marriage with Albert, Nettie comments, "It's like seeing you [Celie] buried", to which Celie responds, "It's worse than that" (19). Albert exploits his authority to persecute Celie without any remorse. He beats Celie and glorifies his prejudicial male values to justify his misdeeds. He acts ignorant towards Celie's sexual preferences while having intercourse with her as well. One day, Albert responds to his son Harpo's question regarding Albert's physical abuse of Celie, which reveals his corrupted ideology. Albert replies that he considers himself fair-minded enough to beat Celie for her stubbornness, as she is his wife (23). Hamer and Neville claim, "[…] poor black women are more likely to be sexually harassed, beaten and raped […] because they lack resources to escape the violence inflicted upon them" (24).

Albert suggests that Harpo assert his physical power to subdue his wife, Sofia. Albert claims that the wives should be made aware of their husbands' ascendancy and "[n]othing can do that better than a good sound beating" (Walker 35). Therefore, Albert ensures the continuation of patriarchal abuse through his son. Albert's house does not feel like her own house to Celie. Her statement, "It not my house" (44), indicates that Albert makes her feel alienated, which restricts her individuality. On the other hand, Harpo gets manipulated by Albert and tries to subjugate Sofia. Sofia tells Celie that she has to fight against her father, brothers, male cousins, and uncles throughout her life (39). Sofia concludes, "A girl child ain't safe in a family of men" (39). Sofia's statement can be evaluated as a strong criticism of male stereotypes that obstruct female empowerment. Later, Sofia gets imprisoned "for sassing the mayor's wife and hitting the mayor back" (179). Sofia spends almost twelve years separated from her children and enslaved by the mayor and his wife, Miz Millie. Sofia is mutilated as she refuses to become Miz Millie's maid and strikes the mayor back for slapping her. According to Hamer and Neville, "Institutionalized ideologies of patriarchy, racism, and heterosexualism [promote] a system in which men are privileged over women, whites are privileged over those of color" (26). Nonetheless, the aftermath of Sofia's refusal to become a white couple's maid criticizes white supremacy. Additionally, Albert's previous wife, Annie Julia, is another victim of patriarchy. After her marriage with Albert, Annie Julia's family abandons her. On the other hand, Albert starts cheating on Julia openly and shamelessly while beating her at times. Disgraced and unloved, Julia considers seeing another man who murders her in the end. Contemplating Annie Julia's misery, Shug tells Celie, "Sometimes I wonder what she [Julia] thought about while she died" (Walker 112). Later, Shug suggests Celie to resist Albert's dominance, saying, "You have to git man off your eyeball, before you can see anything a'tall" (177). Therefore, Shug encourages Celie to reject her marriage to ensure her individuality.

Celie's homosexual involvement with Shug and the reconstruction of Celie's understanding of God challenges the presumptuous patriarchal values. Celie's sexual and romantic attraction towards Shug confirms her aversion to men. Shug functions as a catalyst for Celie's sexual awareness. Celie confesses, "First time I got the full sight of Shug Avery long black body with it black plum nipples [...] I thought I had turned into a man" (Walker 47). Referring to her physical intimacy with Albert, Celie tells Shug that she only pretends to feel something when Albert does "his business" (74). In response, Shug observes that Celie remains chaste (74) as she is still unaware of her sexuality. Shug urges Celie to explore her body, and "[a] little shiver go[es] through [Celie]" (75) when she stares at Shug. J.C. Chrisler and I. Johnston-Robledo claim, "The body should be a source of pleasure, the enabler of agency, and the mediator between the world and the self" (11). Therefore, Shug encourages Celie's sexual awareness, which enables Celie to redefine her identity. When Shug and Celie are alone at home, Celie tells Shug about her traumatizing sexual experience with her father in her teen years (Walker 102). In response, Shug keeps Celie in her arms and kisses her tears while Celie cries. As a result, Celie opens up further, tells Shug about Nettie's disappearance, and concludes, "Nobody ever love me" (103). Subsequently, Shug kisses Celie's lips to express her love. It is noticeable that Shug and Celie's intimacy is stimulated by their emotional common ground. Albert fails to establish such a consensus with Celie, which discourages her physical and emotional inclination toward him. Atkinson states, "The 'benefits' [of lesbianism] are, primarily, a relative degree of independence from the institutional alternatives available to women: marriage, motherhood, prostitution" (133). In other words, the solidarity that women form through homosexual intimacy allows them to evade patriarchal oppression responsible for their subordination through mutual comfort and consolation. Thus, Shug and Celie's homosexual relationship depicts an intolerance for male prejudices. On the other hand, Celie embraces a spiritual journey by recreating her understanding of God. Celie's maturation enables her to question God's negligence, and she starts writing to Nettie instead. Celie tells Shug, "[…] the God I been praying and writing to is a man […]. Trifling, forgitful and lowdown" (Walker 173). Celie's disregard for the patriarchal concept of male God depicts one of the phases of her emancipation. She compares God with a prejudicial man who ignores black women. So, Celie's scepticism functions as a resistance against male values. Judy Grahn, in her short poem "You Are What Is Female", mocks the construction of the male image. Grahn writes, "*You are what is female / you shall be called Eve. / and what is masculine shall be called God … now you understand patriarchal morality*" (qtd. in Kaufman and Blakely 160). Accordingly, Shug tells Celie, "Man corrupt everything

[…]. He try to make you think he everywhere. Soon […] you think he God" (Walker 177). Subsequently, Celie explores the spiritual meaning of her existence to deny biblical patriarchy. Additionally, Nettie writes about Samuel and her reformed perception of God to Celie. Nettie concedes, "Not being tied to what God looks like frees [them]" (233). Therefore, both Nettie and Celie subconsciously challenge patriarchy by rejecting the God who impersonates a stereotypical man.

The patriarchal mindset is intergenerational and undermines the individuality of those who conform to male prejudices. Albert's father has ownership of Albert and Harpo's house. As a result, he exploits his authority to control Albert's independent choices. Referring to Albert's failure to marry Shug, she tells Celie, "Albert try to stand up for us, git knock down" (Walker 111) by his father. Similarly, Albert objectifies Harpo and prevents his self-validation. Celie observes that Harpo cannot fight Albert any better than her (28). On the other hand, he blindly follows Albert's instructions to beat Sofia, which eventually ruins their marriage. Likewise, before leaving Albert, Celie warns him, "The jail you plan for me is the one in which you will rot […]" (187). Ironically, the scheme of patriarchy to victimize women often backfires and disrupts the harmony among the black men in the novel. Thereupon, the farcical representation of Albert and Harpo subverts the patriarchal depiction of men. Additionally, Nettie's husband, Samuel, and Celie's son, Adam, challenge the assumed male values. Nettie and Samuel decide to marry as they share "concern and passion" (215) for each other. At the same time, Adam represents a "sensitive soul" (215), unlike the self-absorbed men. Nettie assures Celie in her letter that Adam will make Celie proud (217). As a result, Adam and Samuel offer an alternative to the typical male characters in the novel.

Celie is a victim of male oppression, so she develops an antipathy towards men. Contrarily, Celie appreciates women and feels connected to them as they do not induce fear in her. Celie confesses, "I don't even look at mens [...]. I look at women, tho, cause I'm not scared of them" (Walker 7). Celie fears Albert, but she adores his sister, Kate, his girlfriend, Shug, and Harpo's wife, Sofia. Noticeably, Celie's mother is mutilated by her husband, Alphonso, and dies as a victim. Likewise, Sofia's mother is subjugated by Sofia's father. Referring to her mother's submissiveness, Sofia tells Celie, "[...] she under my daddy foot. Anything he say, goes [...] She never stand up for herself" (39). However, the new generation of women can break this pattern of oppression on them. Celie's transformation into an individual provides an alternative to the traumatic experiences of their previous female generation. Atkinson writes that women need to reject the patriarchal agencies "[...] so that by organizing together, women can create a counter power block to that of men" (105). Moreover, Atkinson suggests that women, "for God's sake, don't get married" (105). Accordingly, Nettie mentions the "friendship among [black] women" and observes that these women "will do anything for one another" (Walker 150-151). Nettie says that the black Olinka women build a support system among themselves as their husbands fail to sustain a mutual relationship with them. Similarly, Celie's friendship with Nettie, Shug, Sofia, Kate, and Mary Agnes offers her comfort and motivation. As a result, Celie rejects being defined by men and pursues her personal goals.

The mutual affection between Celie and her sister, Nettie, serves as one of the key stimulants to Celie's empowerment. Both Celie and Nettie are victimized by Alphonso; hence, their shared misery solidifies their bond. Alphonso signs Celie out of school after her first pregnancy, disregarding her fascination for learning (Walker 11). However, the sisters realize the necessity of education to liberate themselves, so they both study "Nettie's schoolbooks pretty hard" (11). Nettie assures Celie that she "ain't dumb" (11) and requests her teacher, Miss Beasley, to convince Alphonso regarding Celie's schooling (12). Nonetheless, when Nettie fails in her attempt, she ensures home-education for Celie. Whatever Nettie learns in school, she shares the knowledge with Celie after returning home. Noticeably, Celie and Nettie's relationship is reciprocal. When Albert starts visiting Nettie every Sunday evening, Celie advises Nettie to concentrate on her education instead of getting married (6). Moreover, Celie tries to protect Nettie from the same abuse that Alphonso inflicts on her. Suspecting Alphonso's evil intentions to physically exploit Nettie, Celie starts dressing fancy to shift his attention from Nettie (9). Later, Celie willingly marries Albert to protect Nettie, ignoring the misfortune that awaits her. Celie's intention is to free Nettie from Alphonso's grasp, bring her to Albert's home, and manage a way to escape with Nettie (11). As planned by Celie, Nettie flees from Alphonso's home to settle in Celie's place. During her stay, Nettie enables Celie to acquire an insight into the outside world. Nettie ensures Celie's basic literacy skills and "everything else she think [Celie] need to know" (18). Additionally, Nettie encourages Celie to resist domestic violence by letting Albert and his children know "who got the upper hand" (18). Nettie suggests, "You [Celie] got to fight" (18). Apparently, Celie helps Nettie continue her education, transcend female victimization, and follow her ambitions. Likewise, the education offered by Nettie qualifies Celie to communicate her thoughts. The exchange of letters between Nettie and Celie facilitates the formation of Celie's self-awareness.

Celie's written expression enables her to assert her individuality. In the beginning, Celie seeks a rational explanation for her sufferings from God. Addressing God, Celie writes, "Maybe you can give me a sign letting me know what is happening to me" (Walker 3). Her letters to God can be termed as the initial stage of her self-expression. Celie writes letters as she wants to be understood. The idea of having God as a listener provides Celie with temporary relief from her unhappy marriage. Celie tells Nettie, "long as I can spell G-o-d I got somebody along" (19). As Showalter opines, in order "[…] to channel psychic energy, women […] *need* writing as an escape valve for their desperate need for self-expression" (345). Accordingly, it is evident that Celie desires to write down her thoughts to assert her denied voice. In her first letter to Celie, Nettie writes, "You've got to fight and get away from Albert. He ain't no good" (Walker 114). Nettie is aware of Albert's downside, so she encourages Celie to get away from him. Nettie informs Celie that she [Nettie] has received advanced education to join the black missionaries, Samuel and Corrine, who intend to promote schooling in Africa (119). Nfah-Abbenyi states, "[…] women are now writing about women and bringing not only their points of view but lived experiences as women to their writing" (117). Likewise, writing to Celie allows Nettie a scope for self-exploration. Nettie admits to Celie that it feels similar to skipping a prayer when Nettie does not write to Celie; hence, whenever Nettie skips writing to Celie, Nettie feels "locked up in [herself] and choking on [her] own heart" (Walker 117). Certainly, the sisters require a way to interact with each other to liberate their inner voices. Through her letters, Nettie alters Celie's perspective regarding the fate of black women. Nettie enlightens Celie about some existing black people who are not cruel like Alphonso and Albert or subjugated like Nettie and Celie's belated mother (119). Nettie informs Celie that Corrine and Samuel's adopted children, Olivia and Adam, are actually Celie's. Moreover, Nettie tells Celie about Harlem, a territory situated in New York for the colored people. Celie learns from Nettie's letter that the black people in Harlem "live in such beauty and dignity" (121). As a result, Celie realizes that black women have a flexible destiny and she can reconstruct her life like Nettie. Thereupon, Nettie's letters encourage Celie to inspect her present condition compared to that of the evolved black women. In one of her letters, Nettie writes to Celie that Alphonso is not their real father (159). So, Nettie and Celie's interaction through letters broadens Celie's perspective and allows her to discover the truths concealed from her. Ultimately, Celie finds her personal voice and writes back to Nettie, "I don't write to God no more, I write to you" (173). Apparently, Celie prefers writing to Nettie instead of God, as her interaction with Nettie is soul-searching and reciprocal. As a result, Celie's personal growth accelerates when she starts addressing her letters to Nettie as God's replacement. When Celie gets tired of talking to herself, she writes to Nettie (236). Therefore, exchanging letters with Nettie allows Celie to reclaim her individual expression.

Albert's sister, Kate, encourages Celie to acknowledge her worth as a person. Celie's brief meeting with Kate leaves a positive impression on her conscience. During her short visit, Kate recognizes Celie's vitality and comments, "Brother [Albert] couldn't have done better if he tried" (Walker 21). According to Kate, choosing Celie as wife is a sensible decision made by Albert. Besides, Kate convinces Albert to buy Celie new outfits and take her to the store. After purchasing a blue attire, Celie remarks, "I can't remember being the first one in my own dress. Now to have one made just for me" (21), and tries to express her gratitude to Kate. Noticeably, Kate's humble gesture has a lasting impact on Celie. Kate makes Celie feel recognized and instigates a sense of distinctiveness in her. Moreover, Kate assures Celie that she deserves much more from life (22). Kate even suggests Harpo to help Celie with the household chores. Consequently, Albert asks Kate to leave his house when Harpo complains to him. Before leaving, Kate advises Celie to fight Albert and Harpo. Kate tells Celie, "I can't do it [fight] for you. You got to fight them for yourself" (22). Dillon argues, "Self-understanding can be self-respecting rebellion against subordination"; hence "striving to understand oneself is reclaiming oneself from oppression" (64). Likewise, Kate motivates Celie to acknowledge her value and defend her own dignity, as nobody else can support her better than Celie herself. Kate helps Celie realize that she needs to resist her subjugation instead of taking comfort in her confessions to God. As a result, Kate inspires Celie to contemplate her reliance on self-help.

Celie's growing sense of individuality enables her to appreciate Sofia's assertiveness. The day Sofia comes to meet Albert, he claims that she is unsuitable for his "young and limited" son (Walker 31). In response, Sofia asks Albert mockingly, "What I need to marry Harpo for? He still living here with you" (32). Sofia uses her voice to resist Albert's objectification. Sofia informs Albert that Harpo is incapable of providing her with a stable life. Moreover, Sofia rejects Harpo in front of Albert, saying, "[...] Harpo, you stay here. When you free, me and the baby be waiting" (32). Sofia returns to her house, leaving both Harpo and Albert dumbfounded. Evidently, Sofia takes control of her relationship with Harpo, and despite her pregnancy, she decides when to marry him. Furthermore, Sofia has an unyielding personality, challenges Harpo, and acts on her own will. Albert encourages Harpo to beat her, but Harpo's bruised face indicates that Sofia beats him back. Ridiculing Harpo's inability to restrain Sofia, Celie comments, "I don't specs you [Harpo] had a chance to see if you could make Sofia mind" (36). It is noticeable that Sofia's attributes intimidate Celie as she is nothing like Sofia. When Albert beats Celie, she turns passive like wood (23), whereas Sofia fights back against Harpo like a man (37). Driven by jealousy, Celie advises Harpo to beat Sofia (36). Nonetheless, when Sofia confronts Celie regarding this matter, Celie admits to Sofia that she acts on her envy because she cannot do things that Sofia can (39). Celie's confession to Sofia confirms that Celie starts observing Sofia to inspect her own flaws. On the other hand, Celie reminds Sofia of her mother, as both of them are victims of the same hypocritical male society that Sofia is now fighting against. Subsequently, Celie and Sofia find a space for mutual empathy, which settles a sense of sisterhood between them. Additionally, Sofia motivates Celie to resist Albert's abuse by suggesting her to "bash [Albert's] head open" (40). Similarly, Celie warns Harpo that Sofia is one of the women who cannot be physically abused (61). Celie's changed behaviour toward Sofia indicates her maturity. Later, Sofia tells Celie that Harpo's behaviour starts exhausting her as "He don't want a wife, he want a dog" (62). Certainly, Sofia knows that she is not obliged to serve Harpo and leaves him, denying him any control over her life.

Evidently, Sofia's relationship with her white mistress, Miz Millie, contrasts her relationship with the black women. Miz Millie oppresses Sofia solely on the basis of her racial prejudice, bypassing her subjugated position as a woman. Despite themselves being women, the white women usually exploit the black women to sustain their presumed white supremacy, creating an interracial conflict among them. The white women inherit this false sense of power from the patriarchal white society. In this context, Miz Millie receives agency from her husband to enslave and victimize Sofia, a black woman. As a result, the prospect of mutual understanding between women of different races is disrupted. Bell Hooks claims, "[...] white racial imperialism [has] granted all white women [...] the right to assume the role of the oppressor in relationship to black women and black men" (123). Correspondingly, Sofia and Miz Millie portray a hostile relationship. Miz Millie enslaves Sofia and keeps her separated from her children for five years. During Christmas, Miz Millie decides to drive Sofia to her home (Walker 96). However, when Sofia sits beside the driver's seat in the car, Miz Millie makes a racist remark. Miz Millie taunts, "Have you ever seen a white person and a colored sitting side by side in a car, when one of 'em wasn't showing the other one how to drive it or clean it?" (97). Moreover, Miz Millie allows Sofia only five minutes to meet her children before she urges Sofia to drive her back home, even though Miz Millie promises Sofia an entire day with her children. Apparently, Miz Millie threatens Sofia's personal life. Addressing the "white feminists", Hooks writes, "They could pay lip service to the idea of sisterhood and solidarity between women but at the same time dismiss black women" (9). Likewise, Sofia regains her individualism only after reconnecting with Odessa, Celie, Shug, and Mary Agnes. Sofia reclaims her vitality when she integrates with these black women. Sofia's sister, Odessa, takes care of Sofia's children when she lands in prison. After returning home from the white couple's house, Sofia regains her self-esteem with support from Odessa, Shug, Celie, and Mary Agnes. Sofia confronts the mayor's daughter, Eleanor Jane, and tells her, "Some colored people [are] so scared of white-folks" (Walker 240) that they pretend to like Eleanor Jane's baby boy. Sofia denounces white superiority by telling Eleanor Jane that Sofia has nothing to offer but a "kind feeling" (241) to her. Certainly, Sofia reclaims her voice through the agency, which is ensured by her friendship with Celie, Odessa, Shug, and Mary Agnes. Thereupon, Sofia's mutual sisterhood with them confirms the requirement of unity among the black women.

Shug Avery has a remarkable influence on Celie's emancipation. "The Queen Honeybee" (Walker 26), Shug Avery, is an ambitious singer. Celie gets introduced to Shug in person when she comes to perform in the town (25). Celie observes that even someone as magnificent as Shug is not spared from social condemnation. The preacher of the church objectifies Shug without directly mentioning her name. The preacher labels Shug as "a strumpet in short skirts" (42) who sings for money and steals another woman's man. In response to his denunciation, Celie remarks, "Somebody got to stand up for Shug" (43). This is the first time Celie reacts when a man depersonalizes a woman. Nevertheless, Shug has a determined character and challenges Albert every so often. Eventually, Celie starts responding to the exasperating behaviours of men, imitating Shug's assertiveness. When Albert's father visits and dehumanizes Shug, Celie "drop[s] little spit" (52) in his drinking water as an act of resistance. In due course, Shug and Celie develop a mutual appreciation for each other. Celie nurses Shug back to good health, and Shug composes a song titled "Miss Celie's Song" (70) to express her gratitude. Having Shug's song dedicated to Celie provides her with a sense of self-worth. Celie acknowledges, "First time somebody made something and name it after me" (70). Additionally, Shug assures Celie that she will stay in Albert's house until he stops beating Celie (72). Shug's determination to safeguard Celie indicates unity between them. Celie says that her life restarts after Shug's arrival (77). Shug supports Celie in becoming defensive against Albert's injustice to her. Shug retrieves Nettie's letters from Albert's trunk for Celie. Furthermore, when Celie discovers that Alphonso is not her real father, Shug assures her unwavering allegiance towards Celie by saying, "Us each other's peoples now" (165). Shug even reconceptualizes Celie's idea of God to encourage her spiritual core. Shug tells Celie, "God is inside you and inside everybody else [...] God ain't a he or a she, but a It" (176). Later, Shug takes Celie to Memphis with her to ensure Celie's financial independence. Shug assures Celie, "I brought you here to love you and help you get on your feet" (191). Apparently, Shug's only concern is to empower Celie and make her realize her strengths. Eventually, Celie develops a fascination for sewing pants, which she turns into a business with Shug's support. Shug promotes Celie's dressmaking skills, helps her set up a factory, and manages female workers to expand her business (193). As a result, Celie can now employ other women and make them self-reliant like her. Therefore, Shug's affection and support ensure Celie recovers from her past trauma and reshapes her life.

Mary Agnes' maturation after meeting Celie, Shug, and Sofia confirms the significance of black female unity. Mary Agnes is Harpo's submissive mistress. Harpo calls her 'Squeak' instead of using her actual name. When Mary Agnes complains about Harpo's indifferent attitude towards her, Celie advises Mary Agnes to reclaim her real identity, rejecting the one determined by Harpo. Celie observes that Harpo will "see [Mary Agnes] even when he [is] trouble[d]" (Walker 80) if Mary Agnes makes Harpo use her original name. Unfortunately, Mary Agnes gets raped by her uncle, the warden of the prison, when she persuades him to release Sofia from jail. After raping Mary Agnes, her uncle justifies his action by saying, "[…] this just little fornication. Everybody guilty of that" (90). Consequently, Mary Agnes learns to contemplate the nonsensical privilege that men are entitled to and confronts Harpo for his unfair treatment of her. Mary Agnes experiences an epiphany and asks Harpo, "Do you really love me, or just my color?" (90) Harpo replies, "I love you, Squeak," and "kneel[s] down" to embrace her (90). Nonetheless, Mary Agnes asserts her individuality as advised by Celie, and reminds Harpo, "My name Mary Agnes" (90). Within six months, Mary Agnes recovers from her past trauma of her sexual assault and begins to sing (91). Mary Agnes' fascination for singing reflects her desire to ensure a distinct identity. She even forgives Sofia for punching her face during their first meeting. Noticeably, both Shug and Celie encourage Mary Agnes to become self-aware. Intending to motivate Mary Agnes to sing in public, Shug comments, "Listening to you sing, folks git to thinking bout a good screw" (105). As a result, Mary Agnes ignores Harpo's refusal and decides to accompany Shug to Memphis to establish her singing career. Sofia also encourages Mary Agnes to go to Memphis, saying, "Go on sing" (185). Sofia assures Mary Agnes that she will look after her daughter, Suzie Q, when Mary Agnes leaves with Shug and Celie. Therefore, Shug, Celie, and Sofia support Mary Agnes in denying subordination and redefining her identity. The colored women aid one another as a collective to ensure a hopeful future for themselves.

The formation of Celie's integrity involves her own efforts. Celie observes the determination of Shug, Nettie, and Sofia, which inspires her to inspect her passivity. Before meeting Sofia and Shug, Celie normalized her victimization. Eventually, Celie's consensus with Nettie, Shug, and Sofia aids her in regaining her suppressed voice. As a result, Celie's friendship with these black women serves as a catalyst for her developing senses. However, Celie's self-acceptance and her individual attempts are equally important to complete her emancipation. Previously, when Kate and Nettie suggested Celie to resist patriarchal violence, Celie ignored them. Celie considered maintaining her submissiveness as she believed that it would ensure her survival. Noticeably, Shug, Nettie, and Sofia would have failed to motivate Celie if she continued to ignore her misfortune. Nonetheless, Celie finds her will to reconstruct her future alike Shug, Nettie, and Sofia. As a result, Celie evaluates her limitations and rejects male authority to initiate the essential process of her liberation. Celie learns to accept her body, which is an important part of her personal improvement. According to J.C. Chrisler and I. Johnston-Robledo, "People learn about the world and about themselves through their bodies; thus, the body is the basis of subjectivity and self-expression" (3). Similarly, Celie recognizes her abilities and learns the ways to reconstruct herself. Celie confirms the beginning of her empowerment by rejecting her marriage with Albert. When Shug decides to take Celie to Memphis, Albert objects to Shug's decision. Nevertheless, Celie calls Albert a "lowdown dog" (Walker 180) and shocks him as this is the first time Celie uses her voice to challenge Albert's control over her. Celie announces that she is finally ready to leave him and "enter into the Creation" over his dead body if required (180). When Harpo tries to interrupt, Celie retaliates by saying, "Oh, hold on hell" (181) and blames him for Sofia's misery. Moreover, Celie defends herself by "jab[bing]" Albert's hand with her "case knife" when he aims to slap Celie (181). It is evident that Celie is no longer a silent sufferer but an evolved individual. Albert tries to discourage Celie's confidence and calls Celie black, poor, ugly, and "nothing [significant] at all" (187). In response, Celie curses Albert to "suffer twice" the pain he causes her (187). Intending to assert her individuality, Celie says, "I'm pore, I'm black, I may be ugly [...]. But I'm here" (187). Dillon claims, "[...] I believe that personal/political empowerment comes most directly and deeply from claiming one's intrinsic worth as a person" (55). Accordingly, Celie's unwavering sense of individuality ensures her growth. Celie moves into Shug's apartment in Memphis and utilizes her sewing skills to become financially independent. Eventually, Celie inaugurates her own factory named "Folkspants, Unlimited" (Walker 193). Referring to her personal accomplishments, Celie writes to Nettie, "I am so happy. I got love, I got work, I got money, friends and time" (194). Subsequently, Celie renegotiates the power dynamic of her relationship with Albert. He fails to recognize Celie when she comes to visit Harpo and Sofia, wearing "Little red flat-heel slippers, and a flower in [her] hair" (196). Additionally, Celie's actions reflect her spiritual maturation. Celie writes to Nettie that her body is aging but her heart feels "young and fresh" (235). Celie tells Nettie that she no longer hates Albert (235) because he is trying to correct his past mistakes. Celie even accepts Shug's relationship with Germaine. Celie admits, "Just cause I love her [Shug] don't take away none of her rights" (244). Apparently, Celie has her own identity now and requires nobody's validation. Celie tells Albert, "Our own self is what us have to hand" (246) to emphasize her enablement. When Albert asks Celie to continue her life with him, Celie responds, "I still don't like frogs [men], but let's us be friends" (257). Celie unwillingly marries Albert for the first time, but she refuses to restart her life with him after regaining her individuality. Thereupon, it is noticeable that Celie aspires to support herself and requires nobody to define her identity. Observably, one day at the restaurant in Memphis, Celie receives a fortune cookie that says, "[…] because you [Celie] are who you are, the future look happy and bright" (223). Likewise, Celie's reclaimed confidence and self-respect ensure a positive change in her life. Celie regains the ownership of her house after Alphonso's demise. Moreover, Nettie returns along with Celie's children, Adam and Olivia. In the concluding line, Celie says, "I think this the youngest us ever felt" (261). Certainly, Celie is responsible for reshaping her future; thus, she confirms the happy ending of her story.

In this chapter, we have attempted to prove that Alice Walker's protagonist, Celie, subverts male prejudices through the support and inspiration received from her black female friends. Celie's determination and individual attempts enable her to resist male domination and re-conceptualize her identity. Since her arrival, Shug challenges Albert's egotistical manhood. Shug redefines Albert as a frail boy who is yet to become a man. After observing Albert's tendency to dominate Celie, Shug sarcastically expresses her relief at not being married to him. Later, Shug suggests Albert to become considerate towards Celie's sexual desires, and mocks him for acting like a "jackrabbit" (245). So, Shug relies on her wit to demean Albert's hypocritical attitude. Similarly, Sofia injures Harpo whenever he tries to beat her. When Harpo tries to showcase his pretentious manliness, Celie makes a funny remark regarding his failure to subjugate Sofia. Eventually, Celie learns to confront Albert regarding his inexcusable behaviour. Celie identifies Albert's resemblance to a "frog" (230) and mocks his inability to modify his personality. As a result, the parodic expression of the black female characters attacks the presumed superiority of the typical men in the novel. Additionally, Shug and Celie develop a relationship that involves romance and sexual intimacy. It is noticeable that Shug makes Celie feel loved and respected, which is the complete opposite of what she receives from Albert. For this reason, Celie gets emotionally and sexually attracted to Shug. Thereupon, Celie's preference for a female lover reflects on her detest for the stereotypical men. In the novel, Shug, Nettie, and Sofia are assertive black female characters. Celie gets inspired by them to secure her future. Nettie and Celie's exchange of letters allows them to convey their thoughts. Additionally, Nettie, Sofia, and Shug encourage Celie to resist Albert and Harpo's ill-treatment. Similarly, Shug assists Celie in realizing her ignored potential. She supports Celie to become self-reliant. On the other hand,

Celie motivates Mary Agnes to reclaim her original identity, which Harpo attempts to distort, while Shug helps Mary Agnes secure her singing career. As a result, Shug, Nettie, Celie, Mary Agnes, and Sofia construct a mutual support system that benefits them on an individual level. Furthermore, Celie learns to rely on herself to reconstruct her distinct identity. Celie begins her story as a sufferer but concludes as an accomplished individual. Apparently, she makes an effort to transform herself from a victim to an ambitious woman. Celie's friendship with Shug, Nettie, and Sofia inspires her to inspect her drawbacks and regain her self-esteem. Consequently, Celie takes control of her life, saves herself from an abusive marriage and establishes her identity as a businesswoman. As a result, Celie's friendship with the black women and her own efforts ensure her emancipation. It is understandable from our overall analysis in this chapter that the black female characters effectively dismantle the patriarchal mindset through their unity. In the next chapter, we will show how in *Sassafrass, Cypress & Indigo*, Ntozake Shange provides the three sisters with the necessary strength through mutual dependence and association with other black women in society. We will also highlight how Shange uses ancestral spirits and various forms of artistic expression as a means for women to escape both patriarchal and racial marginalization and assert their freedom.

| Chapter 5 |

Searching for Female Identity and Freedom in Ntozake Shange's *Sassafrass, Cypress & Indigo*

"Them whites what owned slaves took everythin' was ourselves
& didn't even keep it fo' they own selves. …
Took them language what we speak."

(Shange 27)

Ntozake Shange's *Sassafrass, Cypress & Indigo* mirrors the inequalities and brutalities of white colonialism inflicted on black people. The history of the Americas is seen and depicted from a (de)colonial female viewpoint. In bringing down different literary genres from oral and written cultures and intertwined temporalities and spiritualties, she connects the experiences of black women in the Americas with the experience of colonialism, slavery with its brutalities such as rape, dominance and male violence. Shange highlights the assertion of female identity and subjectivity and the liberation of women, however, she is well aware of the danger of being silenced again. She offers an insight into the uncertain way of regaining female subjectivity within the heterosexual relationship. By emphasizing the lives of black women, Shange demonstrates the way art – music, dance and weaving – plays a significant role in female emancipation and self-expression, particularly the ways in which music works as a unifying factor among black people. While Sassafrass incarnates black women's heritage with her reconceptualized writing and/or weaving, Cypress does so with her body movements and Indigo with her music and magic. However, the act of reclaiming black women's artistic and political subjectivity is interwoven with an unresolved domestic tension where, by denying the accepted notions of marriage, Indigo overcomes the language of domesticity. Through Indigo's rejection of the reconception of the idea of domestic life, the traditional homeplace metamorphoses into a site of protest or defiance. The subversion of the homeplace is further strengthened by re-examining the historical experiences made understandable through Indigo's magic, which has a substantial root. By depicting the search or struggle for female freedom through spirituality, Shange provides them with a voice against a cruel world that subjugates and silences them. Shange also shows the black slaves' connection with spirituality as a way of seeking solace for their suffering and escaping their bitter lives.

Ntozake Shange's first novel, *Sassafrass, Cypress & Indigo*, tells the (hi)story of the Effania family, showing the individual struggle and development of the Effania sisters: Sassafrass, Cypress and Indigo. By mixing recipes, poems and cartographies, Shange associates each sister's life story with their family history and the history of African Americans. The individual stories of the sisters are set against the historical background of the volatile 1960s and part of the 1970s, a period marked by the 'Civil Rights Movement' and the 'Black Power Movement,' which endangered the foundations of white domination in the United States and advocated black struggle against colonialism in the United States and across the globe. The stories of the three sisters, encountering contradictory expectations, traditions and neo/postcolonial experiences, expose the search for their voice and identity as women, artists, daughters and social and political activists. By (re)positioning the sisters in a constantly changing setting and allowing them to communicate via different means of memory and communication, Shange's narrative connects "storylines through translocational imaginaries of black cultures" (Raussert 57). Therefore, history is internalized in the psyche of female protagonists and is closely associated with a sense of place and culture. The Effania sisters are storytellers and conjurers, possessing great skills of connecting with larger black worlds as in the slave communities imagined by Indigo: "African dolls filled with cotton root bark, so they'd have no more slave children. Jamaican dolls in red turbans, bodies formed with comfrey leaves because they'd had to work on the Caribbean and American plantations, and their bodies must ache and be sore" (Shange 6). Sassafrass's conjuring of a network of colored people, a community of female weavers, connects the histories of both indigenous and black women in America: "Toltecas spinning shimmering threads; East Indian women designing intricate patterns for Shakti, the impetus and destruction of creation; and Navajo women working on thick tapestries" (Shange 92). In order to narrate the mobility and connectedness of Black cultures, various cultural products such as music, dance, weaving, recipes, healing practices and folk beliefs are considered crucial historical and textual sources for the narrator.

Unlike her two elder sisters Sassafrass and Cypress, who leave their hometown for their artistic passion and in search of identity and sense of purpose, Indigo stays back in South Carolina and inherits the historical Black heritage, "[t]he South in her" (Shange 4). By revising her matrilineal legacy as a Black woman, Indigo advocates the possibility of redirecting it as "artistic creativity and political subjectivity" (Kim 3). Furthermore, instead of forming a relationship with a man, she decides to be a midwife "curing women folks & their loved ones" (Shange 222). Her dedication to her job clearly reflects her refusal to be domesticized and suggests a potential option to lead a wealthy life as a black woman. The very first line of the novel, "Where there is a woman, there is magic" (Shange 3), gives us a clear idea about Indigo's character. Indigo's world is all about women, real and imaginary, where she loves playing with dolls, chatting with Aunt Haydee – the Shaman – and visiting Mrs. Yancey and her sister Mary. It is Aunt Haydee who guides Indigo towards her spiritual growth. Indigo possesses the ability to transform the unacceptable reality of black people in America when she attempts to vanish everything that she detests: "[…] she knew the cobblestone streets were really polished oyster shells…There wasn't enough for Indigo in the world she'd been born to, so she made up what she needed. What she thought black people needed." (Shange 2). Indigo's desire to create an alternative world and live in that world enables her to topple the dominant social order. José David Saldívar opines that Shange's act of giving different versions of reality stems from her desire to overpower the existing ideology: "In *Sassafrass, Cypress & Indigo,* she is directly concerned with this different 'version of reality', whose depth and complexity cannot be fully presented by existing U.S. ideological literary labels and categories" (Saldívar 89).

Hilda Effania, the mother of the three sisters, leads the life of a conformist – "interested in family life, children, keeping house, and good company" (Shange 117) – and unintentionally follows the ideological structure that clashes with Indigo's craving for the South. Hilda's oppressive language condemns her dolls as mere childish things – "You're too big for this nonsense" (21) – denying Indigo's magical power. Again, by repeating the stereotype of an oppressed black woman, Hilda destroys Indigo's power over herself: "I'm going to tell you the truth of what you should be worrying about now you such a grown woman" (20-21); "White men roam these parts with evil in their blood, and every single thought they have about colored woman is dangerous" (22). Hilda forcefully imposes on Indigo the twisted identity of black women, which is "filled up with white folk's ways" (Shange 7). Hilda's warning frightens and silences Indigo and "imprisons her in a desirable domain of conventional domesticity, namely 'marriage', which resonates the white-bourgeois norms that maneuvers black women to perceive themselves as easy targets of sexual violence and confine them in the boundary of a household" (Kim 4). However, Indigo shows her strength by ultimately toppling the false meaning of domesticity. By refusing the previously accepted idea of sexual maturity and marriage, Indigo reverses the "language of domesticity" (Kim 5). Instead of accepting her mother's language and the idea of a good life defined by traditional domesticity, she is able to bestow a new meaning on it. She replaces female dependence on male financial support and the concept of physical and sexual victimization of women with her love for fiddle-playing and engagement with dolls, referring to the legacy of black women who stay at home. The reconceptualization of domestic life alludes to Bell Hook's statement on "the importance of homeplace [...] as a site of resistance and liberation struggle" (43). By rejecting the traditional domestic life and reconceiving it from a different viewpoint, Indigo metamorphoses the traditional homeplace into a means of resistance.

Indigo's act of subverting the home place is also rooted in re-examining historical experiences. She turns those far-fetched and intangible stories through her "[womanly] magic" (Shange 1). Here, magic is not unstable or a mere fancy but rather quite strong, understandable and politically motivated as its historical origin is brought forward. To Indigo, it is through the fiddle that the voiceless black slaves get a voice. Although the violin and the fiddle are similar musical instruments, Indigo prefers playing the latter as she believes that the fiddle represents black culture, and the violin echoes the white middle-class culture. Her fiddle-playing seems to bring forth "talkin' wit the unreal" to serve the very concrete history of slavery and to be considered an act of resistance against white supremacy (Shange 28). Her historicized female magic is expressed through her fiddle-playing, giving a voice to many oppressed black people and serving as "many tongues" (28).

The renewed magic and the history of black people are the driving forces for recovering and sharing their collective experiences that would ultimately earn them political agency. Hooks says that Indigo attempts to create a space for regenerating "concrete relational love that bonded black folks together in communities of hope and struggle" (36) by sharing her unique articulation of the black experience, which would provide a "visionary model of black liberation" (39). By filling in the gap between a lost history and her very own black community, Indigo plays a significant role in reforming such common experiences. She "look[s] at a brown-skinned man with a scar on his cheek, leathery hands, and a tiredness in his eyes [and she] ferret[s] out the most lovely moment in that man's life & she play[s] that [the fiddle]," leaving him full of energy (Shange 45). Although the harsh and exhausted demeanour of the man mirrors a sense of loss and weariness, typical of the black life, Indigo's superb and, to some extent, magical fiddle-playing brings joy and happiness, replacing the sense of loss, and "connect[s] soul & song, experience & unremembered rhythms" (Shange 45). Again, by refusing to take money for her musical performance, Indigo seems to say that fiddle-playing is not merely the representation of art but rather a means to address the history of the "slaves who were ourselves" (45). By remembering and revealing the unremembered experiences, she creates a space for a communal bond and unity.

By constructing the importance of black history, Indigo provides Sassafrass and Cypress the space to build their creative skills. However, in a world where black women face multiple means of victimization, artistic freedom is a rare phenomenon. Female black artists searching for artistic freedom find themselves crushed by interwoven sexism and racism, and both Sassafrass and Cypress find it challenging to use their magical creativity to destroy such a barrier. Weaving, which has traditionally been undervalued as a mere domestic skill, is rewritten by Sassafrass as a manifestation of self-expression and assertion of identity. She upholds weaving from "something the family did for Miz Fitzhugh" to some sort of divine art (Shange 70). Miz Fitzhugh's act of engaging black people for their service of weaving, considering it a respectable job for them, relegates weaving to a trade, a domestic slave-craft, and adds a racist connotation to it and groups the three sisters as weavers, erasing their individuality. Shange says, "Miz Fitzhugh liked Sassafrass, the best of the girls. That's why she sponsored her at the Callahan School. The other two, [...] they didn't even want to be weavers. What was becoming of the Negro, refusing to ply an honorable trade" (71). Although Hilda somehow admits the artistic value of weaving, she considers it as a mere "fine craft" (94), again demoting it to breadwinning job. Kim opines, "[...] Miz Fitzhugh's and Hilda's notions of weaving are analogous in reinforcing [white elite norms], for both of them define it as manual labor to sustain a living" (8). However, although Sassafrass admits the fact that she inherited weaving from her foremothers, she asserts her agency and identity by knocking down the white authoritative mode. She considers weaving a form of art which provides "her a sense of womanhood that was rich and sensuous, not tired and stingy" (Shange 92) since tired and stingy are typical of exhausting and purposeless slave labour. Although Mitch, Sassafrass's boyfriend and a strong follower of the Black Arts Movement, encourages her passion for creating blackness, as is suggested by their house motto: "CREATION IS / EVERYTHING YOU DO / MAKE SOMETHING" (Shange 83), he does not consider weaving a representative art form. Mitch's perception that weaving is equal to manual labour, "making things with [one's] hands" (79), deprives it of its creative effort and coats it with traditional domesticity. By confining weaving within a closed domesticity, Mitch, ironically, considers the notion of creation superficial. Mitch's derogatory comments about weaving mirror the fact that "racism and sexism are interlocking systems of domination which uphold and sustain one another" (hooks 59). Kim says again, "Moreover, weaving is disparaged as a relic of slavery that recalls white-male supremacy over black domestic space, robbing the black men's right over it" (12).

For Cypress, dancing plays a similar role to that of weaving for Sassafrass. Unlike Sassafrass and Indigo, who are conscious of their blackness/being black, Cypress initially tries to conform to the authoritative white society through both her verbal and physical expressions. Due to her self-detachment from her heritage, she faces rejection, goes through alienation and finds it difficult to adjust to what does not traditionally belong to her. Hilda's statement about Cypress's choice of dancing only strengthens the racist and sexist attitudes: "Ballet is for white girls; now, can't you understand? Your ass is too big, and your legs are too short" (Shange 134). Not being aware of her racial identity, Cypress is determined to conform to white tradition and "dance as good as white folks and find out the truth about colored people's movements" (135). However, after awakening to her racial differences and redefining the meaning of culture, Cypress starts following "the brazen mystical motions of black Nile dance" (161), where she is motivated to talk about her blackness through the "freestyle Southern improvisations" (161) and decides not to continue ballet and copy the styles and movements of white folk. After she awakens to her racial and cultural identity, "[h]er dance takes on the essence of the struggle of colored Americans to survive their enslavement" (136). During her mythical and mystical performance with the Kushties, a group that follows the political agenda of black people, cherishes African culture and envisages its mythical quality, the border between the dancers and the spectators gets blurred as Shange writes, "The audience doesn't exist; everybody is moving" (114). The unifying image of dancing black bodies is pushed to an intensely magical/mythic state where the magical art of black women demands to be integrated with this mythical notion of black nationhood.

It is only after Cypress is motivated by the "music from home" that her dance eventually comes to terms with her sense of self as a black woman (Shange 156). She uses the magic of her Southern music as a means to express herself:

> *[Cypress] had leaped to the front of the musicians and was speaking of beauty and love in her body. Cypress danced her ass off, [...] Cypress moved as Yanvallou. Curved and low to the ground, her back undulated like Damballa's child must. ... Cypress was a dance of a new thing, her own spirit loose, fecund, and deep. (156)*

Cypress's incarnation of the black women's heritage through her body movement, something that Sassafrass does with her reconceived weaving and/or writing, and her invocation of the history as "Yanvallou" and "Damballa's child" reflect the Southern magic traditions of Indigo, suggesting the fact that Cypress is able to come to terms with her previously ignored legacy and direct it to recover her artistic self and identity. It is through her dance that she speaks up, breaking her earlier silence. Kim opines, "The black ancestral power exerting influence on Cypress celebrates Black womanhood and brings her rich spirit to the fore" (17). She metamorphoses into "sechita, [the] Egyptian goddess of creativity, [who] record[s] [black women's] history" with her body movement (Shange 24). Kim says again, "Cypress's dance moves on from an expression of supposed blackness to femaleness, and eventually to a black woman's selfhood" (17).

In *Sassafrass, Cypress & Indigo,* Shange attempts to defend her own culture and the critical voices within her society. By writing about slavery, Shange aims to recognize, reimagine and rewrite the past to express her views on the value of freedom. Shange "approaches slavery in order to denounce its terrible consequences and show that the values imposed by Western civilization represent a real threat to and even death of so many displaced, vulnerable, and defenceless Black people as well as indigenous people" (Sousa 3). Shange also deals with the notion of spirituality, highlighting the slaves' need to connect to the spiritual world as a way to get rid of their sordid lives. Shange's approach to slavery and her endeavour to keep alive the memory and legacy of the slaves and its cultural features in the South are embodied by the character of Indigo. It is through Indigo that the past and the present are intertwined as she embodies her slave ancestors and their inhabited spaces or environments. Again, the three sisters illustrate the concept of 'Sankofa', meaning coming back and recuperating, as they come back to their original selves and recuperate their African spirituality or mysticism. They also show the same sense of unification and spirituality when they follow a West African ritual of throwing food and drink into the sea:

> *"Wd toss nickels food & wine in the sea down the coast/ so daddy wd have all he needed to live a good life in the other world. A little before, Cypress asserts daddy was a seaman/ a ship's carpenter; he was always goin' round the world/that what mama said/ & he died in the ocean off a Zanzibar/that's what mama said the ship just caught fire /& went on down to the bottom of the ocean." (Shange 97)*

The ritual of giving food to the dead might stand for the subversion of the binary between the dead and the living and, thus, a way to challenge the dominant tradition of the West. The reference to the death of the father of the three sisters reminds us of the millions of slaves who lost their lives in the trans-Atlantic slave trade. Wardi writes, "Shange, like others in the tradition, continues the trope of sea water as ancestrally embodied, consecrated, and divinized, made sacred by those who eternally rest on the ocean floor" (134).

Just like religion, music is also intertwined with slavery, where both represent freedom and escape from daily brutalities. Paul Gilroy states, "[A]rt, particularly in the form of music and dance, was offered to slaves as a substitute for the formal political freedoms they were denied under the plantation regime" (56). It is through the character of Indigo that Shange shows the motivating and liberating role of music for slaves: she communicates with slaves via music as they have lost their voice or language. It is through her fiddle that Indigo expresses her mind and spirit as Shange writes, "Indigo sat in her window, working with her fiddle, telling everybody, the wind & all his brothers, what was on her mind, the turmoil in the spirit realm, the luxuriant realities she meandered in her sleep. Whenever she wanted to pray, she let her fiddle talk. Whenever she was angry, here came the fiddle" (28). The fiddle represents music and embodies freedom, identity and the culture of black people, which white people failed to steal from them:

> *Them whites what owned slaves took everythin' was ourselves & didn't even keep it fo' they own selves. Just threw it on away, yaheah. Took them drums what they could, but they couldn't take our feet. Took them languages what we speak. Took off wit our spirits & left us wit they Son. But the fiddle was the talkin' one. The fiddle becallin' our gods what left us. (Shange 22)*

It is important to note that slaves were not allowed to play the drums as slave owners were afraid of slave rebellions. The slave owners were suspicious that through drum-playing, slaves from one plantation would send signals to slaves in other plantations, thus initiating a slave rebellion.

In order to overcome the pain and disillusionment of her broken relationship with her boyfriend Mitch, Sassafrass "tried everything to be a decent Ibejii, a Santera. She desperately wanted to make Ochá. To wear white with her élèkes. To keep the company of the priests and priestesses" (Shange 195). Sassafrass's practising 'Santeria', an African Caribbean religion brought to the Americas by the displaced slaves, explicitly shows her close association with the traditions and rituals of their ancestors in Africa. Again, maintaining a sincere relationship with the spirits of their dead ancestors helps all the three sisters to be sensible and well-balanced, both emotionally and physically. Shange says, "When her father died, Indigo had decided it was the spirit of things that mattered. The humans come and go. Aunt Haydee said spirits couldn't be gone, or the planet would fall apart" (5-6). Their faith and dependence on spirits clearly show the superiority and significance of spirits over human beings. For slaves, their religious association is a way to escape from their daily suffering and isolation. Although Sassafrass has been physically and mentally tortured by her oppressive boyfriend, she struggles to break her emotional attachment to him. There is a reference to the vision of The Lady, a Blues singer, who asserts that she has come to release Sassafrass from her earthly suffering and enable her to fulfil her dream of becoming a famous author like Zora Neale Hurtson: "It's the blues, Sassafrass, that's keepin' you from writing, and the spirits sent me because I know all about the blues [...] that's who I am: Miss Brown's Blues [...]" (Shange 130). The spirit of the Blues singer suggests that she has faith in her ability as an author and thus tries to awaken her trust in herself. Sassafrass's act of living in her new realm, suggested by the spirit, enables her to abandon Mitch when he hits her brutally and thus assert her identity and be empowered.

The lives of the three Effania sisters revolve around the Black music of the 1960s and 1970s and its discussions of cultural legacy and renewal. Wilfried Raussert states, "Indigo improvises blues, soul, and funk tunes on the fiddle, Sassafrass absorbs the female blues tradition as a poet, and Cypress pursues black dance as a career" (59). It is through the imaginary flight of the three sisters that the readers follow the tracks of oral and musical traditions throughout the Americas. Commenting on the Black musical expressions in the Americas, Roger D. Abrahams opines:

> *Not that these black expressive forms are not associated with specific places: the Cuban Habanera, the Samba of Rio, Reggae and Kingston, and the Mississippi blues. However, these are also recognizably vernacular inventions that achieved a place in the transnational entertainment industry rather than providing the kind of cultural reflexiveness that leads to the formation of a patria. (99)*

Abrahams' statement suggests the spread of a larger black community beyond the borders of the nation states. Abrahams concludes by saying, "These musics, and the peoples identifying themselves through them, knit together the entire region, even as they advertise local cultural invention to worldwide popular audiences" (100). By associating her female characters with Black musical expressions and/or traditions, Shange extends the horizon of the knitting of black histories in the novel, thus strengthening black solidarity and "fus[ing] oral, sonic, rhythmic, and written cultural expressions into a narrative that captures the local spirit, transcends local boundaries and creates a trans-local connectedness of black cultures in the Americas" (Raussert 60).

One of the most powerful forces behind the empowerment of black women is music. Shange shows the way in which the Effania sisters define their positions as writer, dancer and musician – "Lilah James, Eleo Pomare, Rod Rodgers, Royal Brown […]. All gonna be in this special gala for that grand lady of black dance, Sevilla Forte" (Shange 162) – goes beyond Paul Gilroy's theorization of the Black Atlantic. Shange instead attempts to create awareness in the readers of the fact that black culture has developed several traditions of sound and rhythm within the Americas. By mentioning Afro-Colombian and Afro-Cuban modern dancers in her previous statement, Shange attempts to rewrite the history of modern dance in the Americas from the perspectives of North and South American Black cultural heritage. Ntongela Masilela points out and criticizes the exclusionist aspect of Paul Gilroy's notion of the Black Atlantic: "Gilroy defines the 'Black Atlantic' as essentially a dialogical intellectual system of discourse between the United States and Europe about the nature of modernity concerning cultural and national identities" (88). Masilela goes on to say, "With such a conceptualization, Gilroy excludes Africa and Latin America […] from the historical parameters of the 'Black Atlantic'" (88).

The novel *Sassafrass, Cypress & Indigo* follows the logic of a web, reminding the reader of the spider-web model of the 'Anansi' trickster figure and draws upon African Caribbean and African American folk heritage to depict the division and reconnection of black families. However, although Shange includes folk elements in her story, she does not narrate Anansi stories. Raussert says, "As narrators and characters need to find forms to adjust to change, to express resistance and to rely upon improvisational skills, they recall the spirit of the trickster Anansi, originally a West African spider-god" (53). Regarding the subverting and rebellious aspects of Anansi spirits, Martha Beckwith points out:

> *Anansi is the spirit of rebellion; he is able to overturn the social order; he can marry the King's' daughter, create wealth out of thin air, baffle the Devil and cheat Death. Even if Anansi loses in one story, you know that he will overcome in the next. For an oppressed people, Anansi conveyed a simple message from one generation to the next: freedom and dignity are worth fighting for at any odds. (n. pag.)*

Shange employs the spirits of the trickster figures, and the web structure provides the Anansi's power with some sort of digression, allowing "translocational storytelling" (Raussert 53) in the text and "What emerge are complex juxtapositions, oppositions, and syntheses of histories, temporalities, and places" (53).

Shange rewrites the history of black people from the point of view of voluntary forms of knowledge production as provided within the domestic arena for centuries. She lets these forms of knowledge move in her narrative from one location to the other, moving back to the past and forward to the future. It seems that Shange joins what Andrée McLaughlin labels an "intercontinental movement of black women's literary renaissance" (xlvi):

> *Transforming political systems necessitates changing human consciousness and human behavior. Hence, Black women bear witness against domination based on nationality, race, gender, class, ethnicity, sexuality, and other indexes of difference. ... Creating a new reality rooted in diversity and equality, women of the intercontinental Black women's literary renaissance are redefining themselves as well as language, images, ideas, and forms of expression within frameworks of cultural continuity. (xlvi)*

By reconstructing the significance of black history, Indigo paves the way for both Sassafrass and Cypress to construct their creative skills. Kim says, "The energy and vitality rooted in the black tradition within the homeplace are redirected as autonomous expressions of black womanhood. The enlivened heritage becomes both physical and emotional bedrock in reclaiming black female subjectivity (7). Consequently, Sassafrass and Cypress struggle in their artistic endeavours. Shange attempts to reimagine, rewrite and recover black history as she is determined to write on the past issues which were excluded or made invisible by white people. She envisions a new path for the black as she never accepts the fact that blacks and whites are not one race as is advocated by José Martí: "There can be no racial animosity because there are no races [...]. The soul, equal and eternal, emanates from bodies of different shapes and colors. Whoever foments and spreads antagonism and hate between the races sins against humanity" (6). By attempting to rewrite the history of the Americas from the viewpoint of the oppressed black people, Shange strongly urges the readers to cast a new look at this history since they are aware of the fact that "Colonization is not satisfied with holding a people in its grip and emptying the native's brain of all form and content. By a kind of perverted logic, it turns to the past of oppressed people, and distorts, disfigures and destroys it" (Hall 393).

In this chapter, we have shown how it is particularly through the storylines of Indigo and Sassafrass that the black American South is interconnected with the histories of Afro-Caribbean culture as a whole. The references to mobility, displacement and relocation, which are the major characteristics of black cultures, permeate the novel and are expressed to depict Indigo "whose lover was the horizon in any direction" (Shange 4). Indigo is also captivated by mobile bodies and entities: "Indigo liked folks who worked with things that took 'em some place: colored folks on ships, trains, trolleys, & horses" (24). This issue of mobility is also significant in depicting her dead father, "who was a man from islands and turned to sea again as he cherished his independence and freedom from racial hierarchies above all" (34). Through the emergence of memories of oppression, dispossession and enslavement on a Pan-American level, there is a rise of narratives of empowerment which glorify Black American artistic creations throughout the centuries. In the next chapter, we will show the way Morrison, in her *Beloved,* brings back a black girl from her death and, through her memory, unearths excluded history of oppression of black slaves, particularly of women. Beloved, who is the representative of black people or their souls, enables the former slaves to challenge official white history and come up with an alternative history of slavery, thus filling in the gaps. We will also highlight the solidarity among black people, particularly among black women, which functions as a survival tactic and enables black people to (re)assert their shattered selves.

| Chapter 6 |

Rewriting Identity Loss and Asserting Female Solidarity in Toni Morrison's *Beloved*

"This is not a story to pass on."

(*Morrison 275*)

The critics of magical realism often express their understanding of the concept in terms of cultural conflict between the dominant ruling classes, especially male and white Western elite, and those who have been devoid of power. In *Beloved,* Morrison uses the magical realist technique to talk about the history of slavery of African Americans from their own perspective, reinterpret the official history of white slave owners, put an alternative history from the perspectives of slaves, and reestablish the identity lost through slavery. She seems to base her magical realism on the belief system of the African American cultural group rather than that of a particular location. Her female characters are doubly marginalized; first, as slaves, and second, as women. She seems to be partially concentrating on an elaboration of female pain of not knowing one's children, of losing husband, of being continually at risk of sexual oppression, and the history that is inscribed in the mental and physical scars that each woman of her novel bears, for example, Sethe is milked and raped by schoolteacher's nephews, Baby Suggs' eight children have six different fathers, Ella's sexual captivity by a white father and son, and so on.

There is a strong influence of African American oral culture and mythology on Morrison's stories, which are adapted from West African culture. Since one important aspect of magical realism is the use of myth, fable and folklore, she stresses African American oral culture to recuperate black historical experiences. "In *Beloved,* black lore, the myths and rituals of black cultures are the most prominent element" (Razmi & Jamali 114). Morrison feels a strong connection with the predecessors who were the holders of cultural essence, and she employs magical realism in order to be able to use black folklore instead of the authorized belief of the Western world. Morrison's use of inherited myths to restore an identity lost by slavery provides her writing a political dimension. Writers like Morrison contribute to the redefinition of the marginal position of African American writers, going from invisibility to visibility, and this invisibility creates an image which is directly related to the supernatural because it portrays the invisible as opposite to the real or visible.

Beloved is conceived and written from the marginalized standpoint of African Americans who are devoid of any kind of social, cultural and political authority. It is the story of Sethe, a female ex-slave who murdered her baby girl in order to save her from the clutches of slavery. Her grief is so intense that it is manifested in the body of a girl named Beloved, the same age as Sethe's murdered daughter if she had been alive. Although the novel is the story of Sethe, it is also the story of all the slaves of the Sweet Home plantation of Kentucky:

Baby Suggs, Paul D, Paul F, Paul A, Helle Suggs, and Sixo. It is the composite story of all slaves and their quest for freedom, and even of those who died in the Middle Passage during their journeys by slave ships. According to Samuels & Hudson-Weems, it depicts the cruelty, violence and degradation – whether the physical floggings or the psychological fragmentation of the black family – that often victimized slaves, irrespective of age or gender (96). The existence of two opposing forces of magic and reality in *Beloved* probably mirrors the tensions between the oppressed and oppressor discourses. Morrison "uses the magical realist device of a revenant ghost child in full bodily form to bring back the memories of the heavily traumatized escaped slave Sethe (Bowers 80-81). By dealing with historical issues critically and trying to cure historical wounds, magical realism in the novel mirrors history and strives to change it. Sethe's daughter Denver, along with the help of Beloved, draws out her gruesome past so that they can go through a process of healing. Morrison's use of magical realism allows them to create history by telling stories to each other made up from the bits and pieces of the past they have accumulated.

In her novel, Morrison re-imagines the multidimensionality of slavery and projects black people's magical superiority of their disgraced condition through a lot of apparently extraordinary day-to-day survival tactics. "As a result, while incorporating supernatural occurrences that appear real and ordinary, Morrison, at the same time, subverts this characteristic of magical realism by rendering the ordinary magical, the real miraculous" (Lobodziec 111). This happens in *Beloved* when a white girl, Amy, sees

Sethe's puffy feet and compares them to those of a dead man whose body she once saw while she was fishing. "Then she did the magic: lifted Sethe's feet and legs and massaged them until she cried salt tears" (Morrison 35). Again, Sethe remembers how once her numb body was brought back to life by Baby Suggs' finger: "Just the fingers, she thought. Just let me feel your fingers again on the back of my neck and I will lay it all down, make a way out of this no way" (95). Paul D's presence causes other people to open up and confess: "Emotion sped to the surface in his company. Things became what they were: drabness looked drab; heat was hot. Windows suddenly had a view. And wouldn't you know he'd be a singing man" (39). Baby Suggs possesses the magical power of multiplying things, especially food items, which reminds us of what Jesus Christ did with His disciples: "Baby Suggs' three (maybe four) pies grew to ten (maybe twelve). Sethe's two hens became five turkeys. The one block of ice brought all the way from Cincinnati – over which they poured mashed watermelon mixed with sugar and mint to make a punch – became a wagonload of ice cakes for a washtub full of strawberry shrug." (137)

One important feature of the novel's magical realism is the passages which hint that certain characters are bestowed with the magical knowledge of future events. When Baby Suggs wakes up to a "scent of disapproval" (137), which she believes emerges from the black community that forsook her, she, at once, experiences a premonition directed towards ultimate tragedy. "Suddenly, behind the disapproving odor, way way back behind it, she smelled another thing. Dark and coming. Something she couldn't get at because the other odor hid it" (138). This premonition comes just before the Schoolteacher, along with one nephew, one slave-catcher, and a sheriff, arrives at 124 in order to arrest Sethe, who is a runaway slave and who resists her arrest by attempting to kill her children. Another important aspect of the magical realism in *Beloved* is the way the characters respond to the reality of excessive violence. Sethe's willingness to kill her own child so that she can preserve her "magical best thing" is presented as the final act of resistance. Again, the presence of Beloved, the ghost of the baby child who possesses magical powers, is also a magical realist event in the novel. She seems to know what Paul D is thinking when he promises to himself to take some investigation about her identity in the town; in the clearing, Sethe is choked by a spirit, and Denver realizes that it is done by Beloved from afar (96) as he knows about Beloved's ability to disappear and reappear as she did one day right before Denver's eyes in the cold house (122). "Throughout Morrison's novel, Beloved hovers in the space where the ordinary becomes extraordinary, where something that should be familiar seems strange and unfamiliar" (Peterson 48).

The undermining power of magical realism originates from the "juxtaposition of objective and subjective realities in ways that call the objective into question, allowing authors to challenge official readings of social, political and historical events" (qtd. in Razmi & Jamali 113). The source of this subversive and transgressive aspect of magical realism in *Beloved* lies in the fact that once the readers find that the category of the real is not certain, then all the assumptions of truth become vague, and once the category of real is suspected within the fiction, the world outside the fiction is made less certain as well. In *Beloved,* we do not find any difference between the spirit world and the material world, between the living and the dead, between past, present and future. In this novel, Morrison, in her attempt to provide the history of the black slaves from their own perspectives to that supported by the dominant power, uses oral story-telling as a source of alternative perspectives on history since the oral tale was often the only way in which alternative version of events survived. The political objective of the text is that the disposed, the silenced, and the marginalized of our own dominating systems can again find a voice. The adaptation of oral story-telling techniques in a magical realist narrative is often complementary and mutually supportive. "In a text where categories between the real and the magical have already been broken down, allowing for more than one version of truth to be proposed, the use of such story-telling techniques which assume that there are multiple versions of a story, emphasizes the possibility of expressing multiple perspectives in the text" (Bowers 90).

The supernatural presented in Beloved is a subalternized reality; it expresses social and cultural oppression, and is related to the gruesome experiences of the African Americans in the nineteenth century US society. "White people believed that whatever the manners, under every dark skin, was a jungle. Swift unnavigable waters, swinging screaming baboons, sleeping snakes, red gums ready for white blood" (Morrison 198). The novel forms a web of unions between the subconscious, the socially and culturally repressed women within a patriarchal society, and the ghost of what Baby Suggs calls "some dead Negros's grief" (5). Morrison states that the history of slavery of African Americans remains unexpressed because of the disregard for dominant and previously slave-owning American culture. The magical realism expressed in *Beloved* is an ethnicized and marginalized world that indicates the huge rift between white and black worlds. White people are unable to see, hear, or feel ghosts, not because they cannot exist scientifically but because they (white people) are the means of oppression and domination. Morrison's claim that magical realism provides another way of knowing things allows the expression of the unexpressed stories of the black slaves that go against the documented history from a European-American viewpoint.

The African American response to Euro-American modernity encompassed black people's reinterpretation and affirmation of their humanity, which white supremacy questioned or even denied (Lobodziec 112). Although Morrison's employment of magical realism might differ from other magical realists, her concern for African-Americans still seems to be quite in tune with important issues taken up by Latin American magical realists like Gabriel García Márquez, for instance, the ideological justification of the dehumanization of black slaves by Western science and philosophy. Amaryll Chanady writes:

> *Magical realism subverts the canons of ethnographic representation. The dichotomization between the non-reflexive primary society and the Western ethnographer's discourse of knowledge is dissolved by a novelistic discourse in which there is an attempt*

> *[...] to represent an indigenous worldview by means of a non-European focalizer. (140)*

In the novel, the character of the schoolteacher is the epitome of Western ethnography and history. While writing a book about the black slave, he measures Sethe's face with a string and asks his students to describe her by putting "her human characteristics on the left; her animal ones on the right" (Morrison 193). In another instance, a newspaper clipping reports Sethe's infanticide where it aims to project black people as immoral, threatening, wicked and evil, but what it avoids is the victimization and the inhuman treatment of the enslaved. Morrison focuses on the intensity of the characters' emotions and thus opposes the disgracing official history of black people; she wishes to say that black people are not evil but rather are the victims of white oppression. One noticeable symbol of black people's dehumanization and victimization is a humiliating and destructive iron horse bit placed in the mouth of the slaves, irrespective of age and gender. Again, the chained black slaves are forced to live on the level of animals or even worse. Morrison gives us access to Sethe's past by introducing the magical character Beloved and enables us to understand the brutality of slavery, which has so long been silenced and suppressed in documented history.

The magical realist work of Morrison can challenge the past and can determine the history of America with the reality of the current time. She can recover the history and undermine it; she can also show the common and mundane as reality and then introduce the world of the spirit as actuality. Wendy B. Faris says that one of magical realism's paradoxical projects is how to be grounded in history but not crushed by it and, alternatively, how to rise above it enough to reimagine it without shortchanging its intractability ("Ordinary Enchantments" 59). By this reimagination, magical realist writers like Morrison can confront existing discussions of power. The focus on the inner reality of the characters' lives through the use of magical realism seeks to portray such history which is sensed as opposed to the recognized or accepted history. Based on the intensity of the characters' emotions, Morrison defies the bias of documented history recorded by the white slave owners, which has, on the one hand, fabricated the slave stories and, on the other hand, silenced many personal histories of the enslaved black people and disgraced them. Her magical realism stresses the distinctiveness of the experience of the black slaves and counters their discredit with a positive vision.

The novel *Beloved* serves the important goal of Morrison to portray the lives of slaves in such a way that has not been done before; it is an endeavor not to portray "what history has recorded in the slave narratives but what it has omitted" (Samuels & Hudson-Weems 96). Although these slave narratives vividly portray the cruelty, heinousness and inhumanity, they do not want to offend the white audience by being angry and outrageous, which "makes compromise necessary" (96) and pulls a veil over the happenings. Morrison wants to rip the veil to fill in the blanks that the slave narrative left and, through the narrator, desires to reveal the wrong and to correct the full story, but her endeavor requires that she depends upon the memory of others and that she draws upon the memories within. The readers should not merely know about the horror of slavery but feel what it was like. Apart from exploring the trauma that slavery wreaked on those who survived into the post-Civil War period, Morrison ambitiously attempts an imaginative testimony, through the figure of Beloved, of those who did not survive: those sixty million and more to whom the novel is dedicated. The novel challenges its readers to recognize the unbearable poignancy of the claims of the past – the loss suffered not just by those who survived but also by those who did not. In order to reveal the silenced, marginalized and untold histories of the black slaves, Morrison uses the blend of the magical and the real when she introduces her ghost-like character Beloved and exposes the shocking histories of black slaves, which, by going completely against the authoritative history, starts a new beginning. According to Ashraf Rushdie:

> *Perhaps the greatest achievement of Morrison's novel is that she gives the murdered victim of history 'voice'; she resurrects the unjustly killed and allows the daughter to have renewed historical life by criticizing the sort of history that has hitherto excluded her and her rebellious spirit. … In giving that 'ghost' a renewed voice and life, Morrison not only criticizes the institution responsible for Beloved's death but also shows the healing knowledge that accrues to those attentive to the ghost's presence. What Morrison does in Beloved is to remember in order to revive, to survive, to rename, and to repossess. (61)*

Morrison knows that the history of the slaves, from their own standpoint, has remained unexpressed due to the dominant American and former slave-owning culture. The process of writing *Beloved* was difficult and full of hindrances, not only due to her own aversion to writing about slavery but also due to the national amnesia on the subject. In an interview with Time magazine, she says, "I thought this has got to be the least read of all the books I've written because it is about something that the characters don't want to remember, I don't want to remember, black people don't want to remember, white people don't want to remember. I mean, it's a national amnesia" (qtd. in Matus 103). People want to forget the issue of slavery, and the problem emerges from the inability to the complete recognition of slavery, which can be found in the fragmented memories of the daily life that haunt individuals and groups. Morrison says, "There is a necessity for remembering the horror, but [...] in a manner in which it can be digested, in a manner in which the memory is not destructive. The act of writing the book, in a way, is a way of confronting it and making it possible to remember" (qtd. in Matus 32). In *Beloved,* Morrison seeks to find and expose a truth about "the interior life of people who didn't write it which does not mean that they didn't have it"; to "fill in the blanks that the slave narrative left"; to "part the veil that was frequently drawn"; and to "implement the stories that she had heard" (qtd. in Samuels & Hudson-Weems 97). For Morrison, writing about Sethe and the black community was more than a psychological exercise, acted upon by the imagination, to turn thoughts into art. It was, through the inclusion of her memories, an act of writing a part of herself into the narrative, the result of which is a view of slavery unheard before; she claims that the characters are her entrance into her own interior life.

In many ways, *Beloved* depends on the tradition of ghost stories: the haunted house, noises, smells, lights, displaced objects, an ominous atmosphere, and the perception and fear of a dog to the presence of ghosts. The supernatural character Beloved possesses many typical characteristics of ghosts, which include "new skin marked only by the scars of her violent death, supernatural strength, the ability to change shape and form at will and to cast a spell on others" (Matus 114). But the presence of a ghost in Sethe's house at 124 is shown as if it were a normal and mundane event. When Paul D walks into a pool of red and undulating light and feels a wave of grief come over him, Sethe explains to him, in an unastonished tone as if it were the simplest event on the earth, that the presence is the sad specter of her dead baby, whose throat was cut before it was two years old. Morrison employs the magical realist device of a ghost child, who later is transformed into a human form, to return the memories of intensely disturbed Sethe, for whom rememory provides the key to unlocking and transforming a past that has been suppressed by her logical memory. The expression of the past in the form of Beloved causes the characters to recuperate their memories and tell their stories. The presence of Beloved as a ghost is oppositional in the novel because "it bothers the scientific and materialist assumptions of Western modernity that reality is knowable, predictable and controllable" (Zamora 498). By bringing this ghost, Morrison deals with the damned heritage of slavery, and by placing Beloved's spirit in the body of a woman who died on one of the slave ships in the 'Middle Passage', she clearly relates her to all the men and women who were enslaved and the Sixty Million and more Africans who were killed during the passage from liberty to slavery. In her broken memory, Beloved recalls that she is the only one left on the ship after everybody is taken away, and then she is raped. She considers herself breaking into pieces and plunges into the water to meet the woman she is separated from (Probably her mother). In her novel, Morrison takes this ancestor into consideration so that she can speak to the living about the cruel and inhuman treatment black people received at the hands of the whites.

Sethe and others are hunted by Beloved because of their failure to express the history of slavery. Her arrival gradually releases a chain of restrained memories in Sethe, who starts remembering her mother and the earrings Mrs. Garner gave her and also shares these untold stories with Beloved and Denver and, to some extent, Paul D, who begins to remember Alfred, Georgia and a rooster named Mister. The arrival of Beloved produces a transformation in Sethe which allows her to speak the most unspeakable things in her life and thus allows her to reveal the past story, especially the cruelty of slavery, which has been excluded in the white slave-owners history and which is unknown to general people. "Like the historian, Sethe is able to 're-enact' or 're-think' a critical moment from the past and is consequently able to demonstrate her possession 'of' rather than 'by' the past and to alter her own life history […]. It is precisely the (re)configuration of the past that enables her to refigure the future" (Henderson 99). Beloved also arouses memories in Denver as she remembers going to school for one year at Lady Jones' house until she was asked about her mother.

Like other ex-slaves, Sethe wants to remember the past but fails to do so because of the brutality it possesses; she wants to forget but fails as she always lives in the past. The magical realist instrument with which Beloved helps Sethe assert her identity and heal the rift between her and the black community also enables them to form their communal identity. Sethe and other black people in the community are dissociated from the past so that they can forget the brutal treatment they got in the past, and this desire ultimately causes a fragmentation of self and a loss of true identity. Morrison thematizes the unwillingness of the community to confront the past directly in two significant ways: first, by having the events of eighteen years earlier, which resulted in a remorseless confrontation between Sethe and her neighbors; the novel emphasizes that no one wants to think about the day when the community did not warn Sethe of Schoolteacher's appearance at 124 Bluestone Road. Second, in the final pages of the novel, the narrative voice mirrors how quickly Beloved is forgotten: "Disremembered and unaccounted for, she cannot be lost because no one is looking for her" (Morrison 274). Morrison introduces Beloved as a magical realist instrument who, by reminding Sethe and other ex-slaves of their past, ultimately helps them reassert their identity and fill the void in their selves.

The theoreticians and practitioners of magical realism also emphasize the important role of community. Faris says,

"Magic is communal" (183), and Faris and Zamora write that Magical realist texts "may encode the strengths of communities even more than the struggle of individuals. Societies, rather than personalities, tend to rise and fall in magical realist fiction" (10). In *Beloved,* Morrison describes the communal unity during slavery and its aftermath, where black people, particularly black women, through their experiences, responded to the modern world not only as individuals but also as a group, a community. "The black women, gathered in front of 124, transform themselves by the sound of their singing into a powerful black church that liberates Denver and Sethe from the oppressive spiritual presence of Beloved" (Lobodziec 116). Lady Jones devotes her entire life to educating the unpicked and the unprivileged, and, in order to help Sethe and Denver, she invites other black people of the community who share their food with the helpless mother and daughter. Again, as a chain-gang prisoner, Paul D needs the support of the other forty-five men for his survival. All these events emphasize the importance of community in the novel.

Despite critical attempts to fix Beloved's identity as Sethe's daughter or as an imposter, it seems clear enough that the ghost is a layering of unstable and suggestive identities, whose fundamental unknowability is the very point. "Beloved may be effectively linked to the Freudian concept of the 'return of the repressed': literally, she returns as the murdered daughter who has been forgotten by the community, but she also represents other memories that Paul D and Sethe have successfully repressed for years" (Peterson 49). The return of the repressed can result in eye-opening, disturbing moments of recognition, and indeed, this happens in *Beloved* as the initial part draws to a close and everything seems to be falling apart. Morrison wants her characters to remember their past and the inhuman treatment of the slaves, and Beloved's presence and influence make possible a necessary but painful reckoning with the past, bringing to consciousness the tragedies and brutalities of slave systems. Beloved does not merely symbolize the spirit of Sethe's daughter; she also stands for the subdued collective memory of violated people and literally and symbolically becomes the internal language of the pain externalized. Karla Halloway reads Beloved's connection to enormous suffering not only as an overwhelming loss but also as the prospect of healing:

> *If Beloved is not only Sethe's dead daughter returned, but the return of all the faces, the faces of mothers and their children who have lost their being because of the force of [...] Euro-American slave history, then she has become a cultural mooring place, a moment for reclamation and for renaming. (qtd. in Peterson 54)*

Morrison creates a bridge between communal and individual memories through the character of Beloved. Sethe tells Denver, "Some things go. Pass on. Some things just stay. I used to think it was my rememory [...] even if I die, the picture of what I did, or knew, or saw is still out there. Right in the place where it happened" (Morrison 35-36). When Denver asks whether other people can see it, Sethe replies: "Oh, yes. Oh, yes, yes, yes. Someday, you may be walking down the road, and you hear something or see something going on. So clear. And you think it's you thinking it up. A thought picture. But no. It's when you bump into a rememory that belongs to somebody else" (36). By acknowledging this collective history and pain, Sethe paves the way for Beloved's obtaining the physical shape in the novel. According to Razmi & Jamali, Beloved's return symbolizes not only Sethe's individual past but also the communal past of the ex-slaves; it represents Ella's child, the runaway captive from Deer Creek, and, most importantly, Middle passage (117). The characters create a bond among themselves through the memories of the traumatic experiences of the past; after getting an opportunity to share history, they recollect and excel in terror. In an interview, Morrison focuses on the effects of the characters' collective memory:

> *No one tells the story about himself or herself unless forced. They don't want to talk, they don't want to remember, they don't want to say it because they are afraid of it – which is human. But when they do say it, and hear it, and look at it, and share it, they are not only one; they're two, and three, and four [...]. The collective sharing of that information heals the individual and the collective. (Taylor-Guthrie 248)*

Beloved's stories and actions suggest that she symbolizes all the children taken away from their families and subjugated in the white culture. She can rightly be considered not only as an expression of Sethe's guilt but also as an association between the individual and the community, as well as the personal and communal history. "The two histories are connected in Beloved's flesh form as she makes it possible to deal with these memories in a way that healing of some wounds becomes possible" (Razmi &

Jamali 118). Later, Beloved is found to be evil and is eventually exorcised by the women of the community. The pain Sethe is experiencing is noticed by the community through the appearance of Beloved; they feel the necessity of standing beside her, helping her get rid of their suffering and asserting her own identity. They see:

> *Beloved bending over, Sethe looked at the mother, Sethe the teething child, for other than those times when Beloved needed her, Sethe confined herself to a corner chair. The bigger Beloved got, the smaller Sethe became; the brighter Beloved's eyes, the more those eyes that used never to look away became slits of sleeplessness. Sethe no longer combed her hair or splashed her face with water. She sat in the chair licking her lips like a chastised child while Beloved ate up her life, took it, swelled up with it, and grew taller on it. And the older woman yielded it up without a murmur. (Morrison 250)*

According to Foreman, "Beloved's most basic premise lies in the magical; it is the community's shared belief in magic that enables them to save Sethe from Beloved's negative effect" (qtd. in Razmi & Jamali 118). Beloved's presence allows the community not only to understand Sethe's sufferings but also to remember their disremembered selves, and seeing Beloved, the singing women confront not only Sethe's past but also their own past. "When they caught up with each other, all thirty, and arrived at 124, the first thing they saw was not Denver sitting on the steps, but themselves, younger, stronger, even as little girls lying in the grass asleep. Catfish was popping grease in the pan, and they saw themselves scoop German potato salad onto the plate" (Morrison 258). Razmi and Jamali state, "In consequence, their images of a younger self, which was caused by the presence of Beloved, let them recognize a spirituality shattered by the experience of slavery. In this way, they are able to call forth their disremembered selves created in slavery" (118).

Whereas in Parts 1 and 2, Beloved symbolizes the past of slavery and the mother-daughter relationship, in Part 3, she becomes greedy, unquenchable, and revengeful. It is quite evident that despite all of Sethe's explanations, love, and attempts to justify her infanticide, Beloved can neither forget nor forgive and can only assert her own feelings of desertion and pain. There is something so dangerous about her desire to take revenge on Sethe that it seems unearthly, and it is Denver who understands quickly that she needs help for her mother when Sethe spits up something she did not eat, which signifies the way Beloved started to possess her body and soul; Beloved is transformed into a witch, a devil, or a succubus. When Denver rushes to the people of the community, they do not want to repeat the same mistake they committed eighteen years ago when they, out of jealousy, failed to inform Sethe of the arrival of Schoolteacher and his team, which resulted in a tragic infanticide and Sethe's alienation from the rest of the community. Besides this, Beloved seems pregnant and "the community of women at the end cannot allow Beloved to deliver a child that would remind them of their forced reproduction under slavery, and so they are motivated to find a way to exorcise her from Sethe's and their own lives" (Peterson 57). Thus, the necessity of getting rid of Beloved and the desire to reorganize the past once again gives the community a chance to amend their mistake, and they decide to exorcise her for the final time. Through Morrison's magical realist instrument Beloved, Sethe and other people of the community become reunited; Sethe is able to reappear from the space of rememory and reassert her identity through the help of other community members.

Beloved's disappearance among the singing and dancing women remains as mysterious as her appearance. The community of black women decides to admit Sethe to their team after a long standoff and alienation of eighteen years, and Beloved, who is a devil child symbolizing greed and vengeance, is unmatched for and unwanted in the community. Morrison represents the return of the repressed past of Sethe, Paul D, Baby Suggs, and other people of the black community through the character of Beloved and forces us to face the historical past as a living and spiteful presence. Through the demonic characteristics of Beloved's character, Morrison draws our attention to historical atrocities, but "she must be exorcised in order for a history of trauma to relinquish its hold and allow African Americans to go on living" (Peterson 58).

Toni Morrison was not really concerned about a nation, subcontinent or continent but focused mainly on a marginalized community and their struggle against white supremacy. Her *Beloved* is indeed an unrepresentable story told from the perspectives of women, and by using magical realism, she creates a history for these women and for people of the community to convey the real, which has so long been ignored and excluded. In this novel, she employs magical realism as a resistance against the white American culture and history; she uses the technique to rewrite the slave history from their own perspectives and to form an identity lost through slavery. By introducing a magical character with a narrative voice, Beloved alters the established notion of reality in accordance with Eurocentric definitions. This magical character, Beloved, reminds Sethe of her brutal past, which she never wants to remember, enables her to create her history, which has largely been ignored in the white slave-owners' version of history, and helps her form an identity. The character Beloved herself is a magical realist device used by Morrison to make the absence of past slavery present and to deal with the bloody legacy of slavery. By linking Beloved to all males and females who died in the 'Middle Passage', Morrison actually represents her as both the individual and the communal past and the representative of the marginalized and the disempowered. Through Sethe and the community's remembrance and knowledge of the past and a sense of identity, Morrison provides an alternative history from the perspective of the slaves.

| Chapter 7 |

Conclusion

Our research aims to address the elements that can facilitate the individual interests of marginalized black women. Black women face racial and gender-based stereotypes that position them below white women in society. Therefore, it is important to address the social factors that impede black women's interpersonal development and find an answer to how their subjectivity can be re-established. In this book, we have conducted our research on five novels that are written by black female authors about the marginalized black female protagonists to disrupt the patriarchal narrative and provide an authentic representation of black women's experiences. For our research, we have incorporated several theoretical lenses and established arguments to support the progressive impact of black sisterhood delineated in these texts.

In the second chapter of the book, we have utilized the theoretical viewpoints of gynocriticism and black feminism to analyze how Tituba's first-person narrative dismantles male diction and assists her in reclaiming individuality in *I, Tituba, Black Witch of Salem*. Moreover, we have used the critical lenses of magical realism and magical feminism to argue that female friendship enables the victimized black women to avoid repeating the past mistakes of their female ancestors and reconstruct their fate as a collective. In this novel, Tituba is repeatedly traumatized by the hypocritical Puritan community and men. However, she uses her magical ability to transcend the attempts of the patriarchal society to derogate and subjugate her. Tituba's connection with her female ancestors enables her to learn from their past and get motivated to disrupt the cycle of violence against black women. Our research in this chapter has attempted to argue that the fictional Tituba gets the chance to evade the Salem Witch Trial, unlike the historical Tituba, as she (the fictional Tituba) receives support from other black female characters. Tituba attempts to connect with black female predecessors and descendants through magic and succeeds in building an effective resistance against male violence.

To keep our research specific and relevant, we did not consider several arguments and interpretive approaches in this paper. Although a plethora of research has already been conducted on *I, Tituba, Black Witch of Salem,* this text can still be assessed from other analytical standpoints. The novel mocks the hypocritical society by reconstructing historical Tituba's story and we have focused on fictional Tituba's challenges as a black slave woman in the paper. However, the focus can also be shifted to the black female author to evaluate the experiences of black female writers in a hegemonic society that shows preference towards male writings. For example, the text briefly includes Hester, an educated black woman who fails to survive the scrutiny of male privilege. While talking to Tituba, Hester refers to Milton's *Paradise Lost* and expresses her desire to write a book about an ideal society operated by women. Despite her fascination towards literature and writing, Hester commits suicide to escape her misfortune caused by the male-dominated society. Future research can compare Hester to modern black female writers to investigate whether they succeed in writing subversive literature or get pressurized to satisfy the expectations of patriarchal society through their writing.

Our research in the third chapter critically explores whether a progressive male-female relationship can be ensured if men do not conform to patriarchy. Additionally, we have attempted to analyze whether or not a heterosexual relationship always promotes the objectification of women. We have used the theoretical perspective of black feminism to analyze Cocoa's marriage with George in *Mama Day*. Cocoa pursues her dreams even after marriage without facing patriarchal barriers, as her relationship with George does not comply with patriarchal ideologies. Furthermore, we have used the critical lens of magical realism to assess how Miranda uses her magic to salvage Cocoa and argue that black female unity is an indispensable element in rehabilitating black women's repressed identity. Additionally, our research in this chapter incorporates Springer's concept of female jealousy to investigate how the absence of friendship between Ruby and Cocoa impedes their growth. Cocoa's life is threatened by Ruby's malice and regains its vitality through the support she (Cocoa) receives from Miranda and Abigail. The shared sense of solidarity between Cocoa, Miranda, and Abigail offers Cocoa a support system that she utilizes to overcome her obstacles.

To conduct the research on *Mama Day*, we have mainly analyzed the significance of Cocoa's shared empathy with Miranda and Abigail to rehabilitate Cocoa's future. Moreover, we have demonstrated how Cocoa's marriage with George subverts masculinity and facilitates Cocoa's personal development during her stay in New York. There are scopes to evaluate the text from other argumentative viewpoints. For instance, Cocoa is a black female incomer in New York who struggles for years to adjust to the white community. Cocoa succeeds in adjusting to the foreign environment only after meeting George, a man of her own race. Further research can be done to investigate whether or not Cocoa feels more connected with her own people, George, Miranda and Abigail, as she is a reject in the white community. Future research can explore how Cocoa's struggles in New York echo the recent experiences of black female settlers who receive fewer privileges than native white women due to their African ethnicity.

In the fourth chapter of the book, we have incorporated the theoretical perspective of gynocriticism to assess how the letters written by Celie and Nettie allow them an agency to assert their voices in *The Color Purple*. We have used Krefting's critical viewpoint on female humour to argue that the satirical remarks made by the black female characters challenge presumed masculinity in the text. In an attempt to deny their male partners any opportunity to objectify them, Celie, Shug and Sofia often make sarcastic remarks to intimidate the manliness of their male partners. Moreover, we have analyzed Celie's attraction towards women through the theoretical lens of female homosexuality and attempted to prove that Celie's sexual involvement with Shug functions as one of her (Celie's) strategies to deny male influence. The black female characters in the text embrace distinctive strategies to subvert male assumptions and assert their individuality. Since Celie detests men and fails to connect with them, she develops affection towards Shug. Furthermore, we have utilized Hamer and Neville's observations on black women's mutual empathy as a theoretical basis to argue that the black female characters in the text find their struggles in a patriarchal society as a mutual ground to develop alliances and revitalize as a collective. We have also incorporated Dillon's perspective on self-respect to denote how Celie's female friends serve as a motivating force for her to regain self-worth and take the initiative to reconstruct her identity. Celie's emancipation is determined by self-aid and her friendship with other black female characters. Celie's friends encourage her to alter her fate and she herself puts an effort to ensure it.

We have concentrated on Celie's friendship with other black women and the diverse strategies she employs to protect her individuality. Moreover, we have critically interpreted Celie's romantic and sexual attraction towards Shug to argue that her homosexual behaviour acts as one of the methods to resist male influence in her life. There is still more room to explicate Celie's homosexuality from other analytical points of view. Celie's acceptance of her homosexual identity plays a significant role in her emancipation. It enables her to reject Albert and take control of her partner's preference. Further research can be done to inquire whether or not the novel's homosexual references encourage lesbian black women to accept their queer identity and disrupt the heteronormative ideas that benefit men in society.

In the fifth chapter of the book, we have explored the way Shange reimagines and rewrites the history of African Americans in *Sassafrass, Cypress & Indigo,* giving them their voice and identity and therefore unearthing the excluded pasts. It is Indigo who makes it possible for her two sisters, Sassafrass and Cypress, to construct their artistic skills by restructuring the significance of the history of black people. By filling in the gap between a lost history and her very own black community, Indigo plays a significant role in reforming many common black experiences which have the potential to offer them liberation. Shange shows the individual struggle and development of the three Effania sisters and associates their individual stories with the family history and the collective history of African Americans. As storytellers and conjurers, the three sisters are connected with the larger black world, which ultimately gives them the necessary strength to survive both gendered and racial marginalization. It is Sassafrass's conjuring of the community of female weavers which connects the histories of both indigenous and black women in America. Again, to Indigo, it is the fiddle, a musical instrument very similar to the violin, which provides the voiceless black people with some sort of voice and identity. Music is thus not only an artistic means but also a means of political protest.

In the sixth and final chapter of our work, we have shown how Morrison in *Beloved* presents an unrepresentable story of slavery told from the perspectives of women and how, by using magical realism, she creates a history for these women and for people of the community to convey the unearthed histories which have so long been ignored and excluded. In this novel, she employs magical realism as a resistance against the white American culture and history; she uses the technique to rewrite the slave history from their own perspectives and to form an identity lost through slavery. The magical character Beloved reminds Sethe of her brutal past, which she never wants to remember, enables her to create her history, which has largely been ignored in the white slave-owners' version of history, and helps her form an identity. The character Beloved herself is a magical realist device used by Morrison to make the absence of past slavery present and to deal with the bloody legacy of slavery. By linking Beloved to all males and females who died in the 'Middle Passage', Morrison actually represents her as both the individual and the communal past and the representative of the marginalized and the disempowered. Morrison also demonstrates the way the (re)appearance of Beloved as a magical figure creates some sort of bonding among the females, and, to some extent, also among the males, of the community, and therefore enables them to survive hardship and to (re)assert their fragmented selves. Through Sethe's and the community's remembrance and knowledge of the past and a sense of identity, Morrison provides an alternative history from the perspective of the slaves.

Based on the critical analysis of the five chapters, we have reached the conclusion that black women need to operate as a collective to disrupt patriarchal assumptions. The authors of *I, Tituba, Black Witch of Salem*, *Mama* Day, *The Color Purple*, *Sassafrass, Cypress & Indigo,* and *Beloved* endorse the concept of black sisterhood as a solution to the predicaments of their black female protagonists. Our findings in this research indicate that mutual understanding among the victimized black women can function as a source of support and encouragement, enabling them to defend their dignity against male dominance. The patriarchal system and white colonialism thrive by controlling the dominant ideologies and social structures, enabling men to exploit women. In these four texts, Tituba is a social outcast in a Puritan community, Cocoa feels alienated in New York City, Celie finds it difficult to adjust in Albert's home, the three Effania sisters are marginalized in a white society, and Sethe and other black slaves are physically, sexually and psychologically tortured at the hands of whites. The prejudicial societies try to constrain their distinctiveness by imposing the predominant rules on them. However, these black female protagonists deny operating within the barriers set by patriarchy. The marginalized and oppressed female characters learn from their experiences and think divergently to disrupt the conventional image of passive women. They emancipate as individuals as they show the courage to contradict patriarchal expectations.

Works Cited

i. Abdullah, Abu Shahid. *Traumatic Experience and Repressed Memory in Magical Realist Novels: Speaking the Unspeakable*. Cambridge Scholars Publishing, 2020.

ii. Abrahams, Roger D. "Afro-Caribbean Culture and the South: Music with Movement." *The South and the Caribbean*, edited by Douglass Sullivan-González and Charles Reagan Wilson, University of Mississippi Press, 2001, pp. 97–115.

iii. Araújo, Nara. "The Contribution of Women's Writing To the Literature and Intellectual Achievements of the Caribbean." *Journal of Black Studies*, vol. 25, no. 2, 1994, pp. 217–230. *JSTOR*. www.jstor.org/stable/2784463.

iv. Arndt, Susan. "Perspectives on African Feminism: Defining and Classifying African-Feminist Literatures." *Agenda: Empowering Women for Gender Equity*, vol. 54, 2002, pp. 31–44. https://doi.org/10.1080/10130950.2002.9676176.

v. Atkinson, Ti-Grace. *Amazon Odyssey*. Links Books, 1974.

vi. Beal, Frances M. "Double Jeopardy: To Be Black and Female." *Meridians: Feminism, Race, Transnationalism*, vol. 8, no. 2, 2008, pp. 166–176. *Project MUSE*. muse.jhu.edu/article/242234.

vii. Beckwith, Martha W. *Jamaica Anansi Stories,* 1924. http://www.sacred-texts.com/afr/jas/. Accessed 29 June 2023.

viii. Blackwell, Frieda H. "Narrative Magic in the Fiction of Isabel Allende by Patricia Hart." *Letras Femeninas,* vol. 17, no. 1/2, 1992, pp. 140–143. *JSTOR.* www.jstor.org/stable/23022035.

ix. Bowers, Maggie Ann. *Magic(al) Realism.* Routledge, 2004.

x. Chanady, Amaryll. "The Territorialization of the Imaginary in Latin America: Self-Affirmation and Resistance to Metropolitan Paradigms." *Magical Realism: Theory, History, Community,* edited by Lois Parkinson Zamora and Wendy B. Faris. Duke University Press, 1995, pp. 125–144.

xi. Chrisler, Joan C., and Ingrid Johnston-Robledo. "Woman's Embodied Self: An Introduction." *Woman's Embodied Self: Feminist Perspectives on Identity and Image,* American Psychological Association, 2018.

xii. Cixous, Hélène, et al. "The Laugh of the Medusa." *Signs,* vol. 1, no. 4, 1976, pp. 875–893. *JSTOR.* www.jstor.org/stable/3173239.

xiii. Condé, Maryse. *I, Tituba, Black Witch of Salem.* 1992. University of Virginia Press, 2009.

xiv. Cowart, David. "Matriarchal Mythopoesis: Naylor's Mama Day." *Philological Quarterly,* vol. 77, no. 4, 1998, p. 439–459. *Gale Literature Resource Center.* gale.com/apps/doc/A60578299/LitRC. Accessed 20 May 2022.

xv. Dillon, Robin S. "Toward a Feminist Conception of Self-Respect." *Hypatia*, vol. 7, no. 1, 1992, pp. 52–69. *JSTOR*. www.jstor.org/stable/3810133.

xvi. Drew, Allison. "Female Consciousness and Feminism in Africa." *Theory and Society*, vol. 24, no. 1, 1995, pp. 1–33. *JSTOR*. www.jstor.org/stable/657918.

xvii. Dreyer, Yolanda. "Women's Spirituality and Feminist Theology: A Hermeneutic of Suspicion Applied to 'Patriarchal Marriage.'" *HTS Teologiese Studies/ Theological Studies*, vol. 67, no. 3, 2011, pp. 52–57. https://doi.org/10.4102/hts.v77i2.6731.

xviii. Dukats, Mara L. "A Narrative of Violated Maternity: *Moi, Tituba, sorcière ... Noire de Salem.*" *World Literature Today*, vol. 67, no. 4, 1993, pp. 745–750. *JSTOR*. www.jstor.org/stable/40149573.

xix. Faris, Wendy B. "Scheherazade's Children: Magical Realism and Postmodern Fiction." *Magical Realism: Theory, History, Community,* edited by Lois Parkinson Zamora and Wendy B. Faris. London: Duke University Press, 1995, pp. 163–190.

xx. ---. *Ordinary Enchantments: Magical Realism and the Remystification of Narrative*. Vanderbilt University Press, 2004.

xxi. Gilroy, Paul. *The Black Atlantic: Modernity and Double Consciousness*. Verso, 1993.

xxii. Hall, Stuart. "Cultural Identity and Diaspora." *Identity: Community, Culture, Difference,* edited by Jonathan Rutherford, Lawrence & Wishart, 1990, pp. 222–237.

xxiii. Hamer, Jennifer, and Helen Neville. "Revolutionary Black Feminism: Toward a Theory of Unity and Liberation." *The Black Scholar*, vol. 28, no. 3/4, 1998, pp. 22–29. *JSTOR*. www.jstor.org/stable/41068802.

xxiv. Hart, Patricia. *Narrative Magic in the Fiction of Isabel Allende*. Associated University Press, 1989.

xxv. Henderson, Mae G. "Toni Morrison's Beloved: Re-Membering the Body as Historical Text." *Toni Morrison's Beloved: A Casebook*, edited by William L. Andrews and Nellie Y. Mckay. Oxford University Press, 1999, pp. 79–106.

xxvi. Hooks, bell. *Ain't I a Woman: Black Women and Feminism*. Pluto Press, 1982.

xxvii. ---. *Yearning: Race, Gender, and Cultural Politics*. South End Press, 1990.

xxviii. Johnson, Michael P. "Patriarchal Terrorism and Common Couple Violence: Two Forms of Violence against Women." *Journal of Marriage and the Family*, vol. 57, no. 2, 1995, pp. 283–294. *JSTOR*. https://doi.org/10.2307/353683.

xxix. Kaufman, Gloria J., and Mary K. Blakely. *Pulling Our Own Strings: Feminist Humor & Satire*. Indiana University Press, 1980.

xxx. Kim, Nayoung. "Between the Magical Legacy and a Model Household: Establishing Alternative Modes of Speaking in Ntozake Shange's *Sassafrass, Cypress & Indigo*." *SNU Open Repository*, no. 36, 2016, pp. 1–24. https://hdl.handle.net/10371/96367. Accessed 27 August 2021.

xxxi. Krefting, Rebecca. *All Joking Aside: American Humor and Its Discontents*. Johns Hopkins University Press, 2014.

xxxii. Lobodziec, Agnieszka. "Toni Morrison's Discredited Magic – Magical Realism in *Beloved* Revisited." *Brno Studies in English* vol. 38, no. 1, 2012, pp. 103–121. http://www.phil.muni.cz/plonedata/wkaa/BSE/BSE_2012-38-1/07Lobodziec.pdf. Accessed 21 June 2019.

xxxiii. Martí, José. "Our America." *Selected Writings*, edited by Esther Allen. Penguin, 2002, pp. 288–296.

xxxiv. Masilela, Ntongela. "The 'Black Atlantic' and African Modernity in South Africa." *Research in African Literatures*, vol. 27, no. 4, 1996, pp. 88–96. *JSTOR*. www.jstor.org/stable/3819986.

xxxv. Matus, Jill. *Toni Morrison*. Manchester University Press, 1998.

xxxvi. Mavin, Sharon, and Gina Grandy. "Doing Gender Well and Differently in Management." *Gender in Management: An International Journal*, vol. 27, no. 4, 2012, pp. 218–231. https://doi.org/10.1108/17542411211244768.

xxxvii. McLaughlin, Andrée N. "A Renaissance of the Spirit: Black Women Remaking the Universe." *Wild Women in the Whirlwind: Afro-American Culture and the Contemporary Literary Renaissance,* edited by Joanne M. Braxton and Andrée N. McLaughlin, Rutgers University Press, 1990, pp. xxi–xliv.

xxxviii. Morrison, Toni. *Beloved.* 1987. Picador, 1988.

xxxix. Naylor, Gloria. *Mama Day*. Vintage, 1989.

xl. Nfah-Abbenyi, Juliana M. *Gender in African Women's Writing: Identity, Sexuality, and Difference.* Indiana University Press, 1997.

xli. Plath, Sylvia. "Mad Girl's Love Song." *Neurotic Poets –The Link between Creativity and Madness,* neuroticpoets.com/plath/poem/madgirl. Accessed 19 May 2022.

xlii. Peterson, Nancy J. *Beloved: Character Studies.* Continuum, 2008.

xliii. Rahming, Melvin B. "Phenomenology, Epistemology, Ontology, and Spirit: The Caribbean Perspective in Ann Petry's *Tituba of Salem Village.*" *South Central Review,* vol. 20, no. 2/4, 2003, pp. 24–46. *JSTOR.* https://doi.org/10.2307/3189784.

xliv. Raussert, Wilfried. "Tracing Afro Diasporic Histories: Translocational Storytelling and Entangled Afro Americas in Ntozake Shange's *Sassafrass, Cypress & Indigo* and Edwidge Danticat's *Brother I'm Dying.*" *Mobile and Entangled America(s),* edited by Maryemma Graham and Wilfried Raussert, Routledge, 2016, pp. 51–72.

xlv. Razmi, Mehri and Leyli Jamali. "Magic(al) Realism as Postcolonial Device in Toni Morrison's *Beloved.*" *International Journal of Humanities and Social Science,* vol. 2, no. 5, 2012, pp. 112–119. Accessed 6 Mar 2014. http://www.ijhssnet.com/journals/Vol_2_No_5_March_2012/11.pdf.

xlvi. Robinson, Victoria. "My Baby Just Cares for Me: Feminism, Heterosexuality and Non-monogamy."

Journal of Gender Studies, vol. 6, no. 2, 1997, pp. 143–157. DOI:10.1080/09589236.1997.9960678

xlvii. Rushdy, Ashraf H. A. "Daughter Signifyin(g) History: The Example of Toni Morrison's *Beloved*." *Toni Morrison's Beloved: A Casebook*, edited by William L. Andrews & Nellie Y. Mckay. Oxford University Press, 1999, pp. 37–66.

xlviii. Saldívar, José D. *The Dialectics of Our America: Genealogy, Cultural Critique, and Literary History*. Duke University Press, 1991.

xlix. Samuels, Wilfred D. and Clenora Hudson-Weems. *Toni Morrison*. Twayne Publishers, 1990.

l. Shange, Ntozake. *For Colored Girls Who Have Considered Suicide/When the Rainbow Is Enuf*. Macmillan, 1975.

li. ---. *Sassafrass, Cypress & Indigo*. Picador, 1982.

lii. Showalter, Elaine. "Killing the Angel in the House: The Autonomy of Women Writers." *The Antioch Review*, vol. 32, no. 3, 1972, pp. 339–353. *JSTOR*. www.jstor.org/stable/4637559.

liii. Sousa, Isabel. "Assertion of Cultural Identity: Slavery, Male Violence, and the Liberating Role of Artistic Expression in Ntozake Shange's *Sassafrass, Cypress & Indigo* and Edwidge Danticat's *Breath, Eyes, Memory*." *Cabo dos Trabalhos*, vol. 13, 2016, pp. 1–18. https://cabodostrabalhos.ces.uc.pt/n13/documentos/06_IsabelSousa.pdf. Accessed 15 July 2022.

liv. Springer, Kimberly. "Third Wave Black Feminism?" *Signs*, vol. 27, no. 4, 2020, pp. 1059–1082.

JSTOR. https://doi.org/10.1086/339636.

lv. Taylor-Guthrie, Danille, eds. *Conversations with Toni Morrison*. University of Mississippi Press, 1994.

lvi. Tucker, Lindsey. "Recovering the Conjure Woman: Texts and Contexts in Gloria Naylor's *Mama Day*." *African American Review,* vol. 28, no. 2, 1994, pp. 173–188. *JSTOR*. https://doi.org/10.2307/3041991.

lvii. Walker, Alice. *The Color Purple*. Weidenfeld & Nicolson, 2014.

lviii. Wardi, Anissa J. "The Cartography of Memory: An Ecocritical Reading of Ntozake Shange's *Sassafrass, Cypress & Indigo*." *African American Review,* vol. 45, no. 1–2, 2012, pp. 131–142. https://doi.org/10.1353/afa.2012.0014.

lix. Whitehead, Ann. "Women's Solidarity and Divisions among Women." *IDS Bulletin*, vol. 15, no. 1, 1984, pp. 6–11. https://doi.org/10.1111/j.17595436.1984.mp15001002.x.

lx. Yavaş, Nesrin. "Gloria Naylor's *Mama Day:* Magical Realism as the Site of Black Female Agency and Empowerment." *Procedia – Social and Behavioral Sciences,* vol. 158, 2014, pp. 247–253. *Science Direct*. https://doi.org/10.1016/j.sbspro.2014.12.083.

lxi. Young, Iris M. "Gender as Seriality: Thinking about Women as a Social Collective." *Signs,* vol. 19, no. 3, 1994, pp. 713–738. *JSTOR*. www.jstor.org/stable/3174775.

lxii. Zamora, Lois P. "Magical Romance/Magical Realism: Ghosts in U.S. and Latin American Fiction." *Magical Realism: Theory, History, Community*, edited by Lois P. Zamora and Wendy B. Faris. Duke University Press, 1995, pp. 497–550.

lxiii. Zamora, Lois P., and Wendy B. Faris. "Introduction: Daiquiri Birds and Flaubertian Parrot(ie)s." *Magical Realism: Theory, History, Community*, edited by Lois P. Zamora and Wendy B. Faris. Duke University Press, 1995, pp. 1–11.